Pilots of Valor

Donald Pickinpaugh

Published by Donald Pickinpaugh, 2023.

While every precaution has been taken in the preparation of this book, the publisher assumes no responsibility for errors or omissions, or for damages resulting from the use of the information contained herein.

PILOTS OF VALOR

First edition. April 25, 2023.

Copyright © 2023 Donald Pickinpaugh.

ISBN: 979-8223180692

Written by Donald Pickinpaugh.

TO REAGON AND LINCOLN, ALWAYS FACE YOUR
FEARS HEAD-ON.

INTRODUCTION

There I was as my arm jerked forward, and a new sensation filled my mind—panic. Thoughts filled my head quickly: today I'm going to die, this is it, this airplane is going to blow up any second, we are sitting on thousands of pounds of fuel (55,000 to be exact), GET OUT!

Imagine flying 500 knots just above the trees when the left engine fire light suddenly comes on. Pilots of Valor takes you inside the cockpit of a high-performance military aircraft when everything starts to go wrong, seriously wrong. We invite you inside the world of a military pilot's day at work.

Military aviation is described as many hours of boredom while occasionally interrupted by moments of sheer terror. This book is a collection of those few moments of terror. The pilots tell some stories and describe how they reacted in the face of death. Some stories recount events in the heat of combat, while others speak of missions that began as routine flights. This book includes ten Medal of Honor recipients from Vietnam. In all circumstances, these pilots put their lives on the line for their country, and, in some cases, they lost them.

PREFACE

As I stepped into the room filled with Veterans, I felt unworthy and out of place. There I stood before men who bore the history of the United States military in their hearts, something I had not earned. Their faces reflected untold stories of honor and hardship, souls linked together by camaraderie and sacrifice. I stood before men whose stories never made it on the front pages of newspapers or magazines. Now, only heroic memories remain. These were moments in time remembered by a few that had long since been forgotten by so many. I have nothing to offer this dedicated group but to share with all their experiences. As they graciously took me under their wing, I felt I did not deserve to be a part of their company. I had never seen what they had seen, nor had I ever achieved what they had accomplished.

My wife saw a man wearing a veteran of foreign wars hat. Having had a father who fought in the Korean War, she took an interest and asked the man what war he fought in.

The gray-haired man, appearing dumbfounded, replied, "What war?" "What war?" he repeated, with eyebrows raised in sarcasm. "Vietnam," came his angry reply.

"Oh!" She said politely, not realizing she had offended him. "I just wanted to thank you for fighting for our country."

Surprised, the man's rigid demeanor broke apart as tears filled his eyes. "Ma'am," replied the gentleman. "Only twice in my life has anybody ever thanked me for fighting for my country, and you're the second."

For these two powerful reasons, I need to share the true stories of twenty men who put their lives on the line for the country we love. With nineteen years of military service under my belt, no honor could be as great as paying tribute to the hundreds of thousands of men and women who have served and paid the ultimate sacrifice for our country. It is now my futile attempt to bring to you a small collection of those American military heroes. In doing so, I would like to thank all who have come before me to fight for our beloved country. I pray that we shall always remember them.

ACKNOWLEDGMENTS

I want to thank my wife for her patience in letting me tackle this project. God bless you. I would also like to thank Major Cory Bartholomew and my mom, Jan Pickinpaugh, for helping me edit this book. In addition, I would also like to thank Lieutenant Jess Smith from Public Affairs for her work in releasing the stories and Major William Druschel from the Legal office for his advice. I am indebted to Major Donald K. Schneider for his previous work on the Vietnam Medal of Honor winners. Large parts of his work show up in this book.

I would like to thank Si Blick from Fox One Studios for the cover art. He has a special gift.

COMBAT

"In Combat, second place is 6 feet under."

Combat, at first, usually brings extraordinary excitement to military pilots. Finally, the opportunity presents itself to go into battle on behalf of our country. Years of training are about ready to pay off. The heart beats out of control on every mission. Thoughts of being shot down or captured are in the back of every military pilot's mind. As time passes, reality begins to set in. Odds, once in your favor, eventually catch up to you.

Twelve Pilots of Valor stories, including the heroism of ten Medal of Honor winners, occur in Vietnam. These men seldom flew the massive formations of aircraft like World War II that pounded Hitler's Germany. Their skills can't be compared to the fighter aces of past wars whose bravery and skill were tested in the unforgiving arena of air combat. The character of Vietnam heroes springs instead from the nature of a unique air war and their extraordinary response to its challenge.

Chapter 1

Captain Merlyn Hans Dethlefsen
F-105 Thunderchief
Medal of Honor

The wild weasel aircraft and crew were well-suited for their hazardous mission. The two-seat fighter bombers carried sophisticated electronic gear and weapons to help the pilot and his backseat electronic warfare officer or "bear" locate and destroy enemy surface-to-air missile (SAM) and anti-aircraft artillery (AAA) sites. The weasel crew was alerted to a hostile radar signal by a rattlesnake-like tone in the headset and a bright blip on the warning scope. They could attack the enemy by unleashing a radar-homing air-to-ground missile from a comparatively safe distance or diving over the site to drop conventional bombs.

The experienced North Vietnamese missile crews could decoy the defense suppression birds by sending all the electronic indications of a SAM launch without firing the missile. With many threat indications, the warning scope would get cluttered. The weasels could never be sure where and when the next SAM would come from. The pilot and bear constantly had to scan the horizon in all directions to find the deadly "telephone poles" rising to meet them. The pilot would put the aircraft into the violent maneuver to evade the SAMs. They feared the SAM fired from a site directly behind the plane might streak in unnoticed to send a lethal blast through the aircraft.

Imagine your flight lead getting shot down while running the gauntlet. You and your wingman are up next and must traverse the same route. What would go through your mind? Major Dethlefsen had one goal. Eliminate the enemy so his buddies wouldn't have to return the next day.

* * *

Outside, the weather was beautiful. Finally, it had cleared up, and we were going after some long-awaited targets. It was the first break we'd seen in many months.

Keeping an eye on the number two F-105, I eased my aircraft into position. I was number three in a four-ship formation. Today was anything but a routine flight. We were going north to Hanoi. Keying the microphone, I announced, "Three's in."

"Lead copies," replied our lead.

Turning my head, I could see number four gaining on us as the green jungles of Thailand fell behind me.

"Kevin, how's our raw gear working?" I asked my backseater.

"Everything's on and in the green, Merl," he answered.

Captain Kevin Gilroy was my "bear." Everybody in the wild weasel business called their backseaters "bear." Kevin had saved my butt on many occasions. While I was trying to find the targets, he was in the backseat, tracking where the bad guys were. Kevin was the best, and today would be no exception. It was our 78th combat mission together.

"Lincoln 10 flight, tankers twenty right," my lead directed, "Two, Three, Four," we all responded.

Waiting my turn, I positioned my Thud under the KC-135 air refueling tanker, as the pilots called it. After taking a full load, I popped back into the formation.

The tanker veered off to the right, remaining in safer airspace as we headed "in-country."

"Lincoln 10 flight, push it up," lead said.

With my left hand, I shoved the throttles up, matching lead's speed. Today our target was over 500 miles away, in the North Vietnamese heartland. The Thai Nguyen steel mill and industrial complex were our new priorities. The area was nestled in a valley 40 miles north of Hanoi and 70 miles from the Red Chinese border. The heavily defended complex was a vital cog in Ho Chi Minh's war machine. Only recently did we get approval to bomb it. We were ready to take it out.

"Kevin, how far are we ahead of the main strike force?" I inquired.

"I'm showing five minutes," he replied calmly. "We'll have to get in and out in a hurry before they arrive."

Now that would be nice, I thought to myself. Get in and out in a hurry. Sometimes it was just that easy, but other times, it wasn't. Today, we were going up against at least one known surface-to-air missile (SAM) site and several antiaircraft-artillery (AAA) guns.

Scanning his gear for the telltale signs that could pinpoint North Vietnamese defenses, Kevin said, "Crossing the border, scopes clean."

"You don't reckon they're sleeping today?" I asked, chuckling.

"Well, if they are, we'll wake 'em up," he replied.

"Lincoln 10, three, and four go one-mile trail," lead called out.

"Roger," I responded as the number four pilot, Major Ken Bell, and I eased back on our throttles. I watched closely as my lead and his wingman became smaller dots on the horizon, almost disappearing.

"Two miles to target," Kevin said.

"All right, let's rock and roll," I replied.

I reefed back on the stick and pulled the jet upward as Ken Bell stayed right on my wing. Glancing at my altimeter, it read 20 . . . 22 . . . 24,000 feet as I rolled my aircraft upside down and pointed the nose straight at the target. I could barely see the lead element a mile in front of us now.

Suddenly, I saw a missile come off the rails from Lead's aircraft, notifying the North Vietnamese we were here.

"Lead's fox four," lead announced over the radio as his missile sped toward its target.

The white smoke trail was barely visible in the intense flak-riddled sky around us. A clear day had suddenly turned black. I saw the impact of lead's missile but couldn't see the final results.

Then the "bear" in the lead ship cried, "We missed. We mis—"

The abrupt cutoff from lead's radio transmission was unnerving. I knew something had seriously gone wrong.

"Kevin, can you see lead?" I yelled while we were screaming toward the ground.

"Negative; I can't see anything," he responded.

Rolling upright, I couldn't see lead or the target as a wall of black smoke was between me and the SAM sit.

"BZZZZZZZZ."

Mike and I recognized the familiar active radar tone in our headsets—the same SAM site we were sent to destroy had locked onto us. I wasted no time as I maneuvered my aircraft down the valley. I rolled left, then right, trying to avoid being hit.

"Merl, lead's hit," Kevin yelled.

I couldn't see the lead aircraft through the flak. I could only see the number two aircraft a mile ahead.

Just then, two broke hard right, and I followed, cranking my airplane as tight as possible. Aching sounds came from my fuselage as my Thud tried desperately to obey my commands.

A moment later, a parachute beeper signal blared on the emergency radio channel. This confirmed that the lead crew had ejected from their crippled aircraft. We were now following the same path lead had taken, straight into the gauntlet.

I saw number two aircraft caught up in a fray of ground fire as he rolled back and forth. He was desperately trying to escape from the hornet's nest around Thai Nguyen.

"Two's hit badly," came across the radio.

"Get out of there," I commanded as number two raced out of the area. Now it was just my wingman and me.

I took control of the flight with the other two birds out of action. I decided we would stay for another pass. Usually, those who attempt a second pass on the target often do not live to tell about it. Still, we had to take the SAMs out of action before the strike force showed up, or they would be vulnerable. I checked my fuel as the gauges read half tanks. We had missiles, guns, bombs, and a job that still needed to be done. I didn't want to come back another day to this place.

Coming around, I studied the flak pattern. It wasn't a matter of avoiding the flak but trying to find the least-intense areas, if there were any. Sometimes we got very little flak at SAM sites, but this was different. I knew this was a vital target by their defenses. Taking it out would severely hurt the North's war operations. Whatever the North Vietnamese had down there, they didn't want us destroying it.

Kevin hollered, "SAM, three o'clock, near an open area against the hillside."

"I got it," I replied, looking over my right shoulder. The SAM radar was easy to identify. Cranking my head further back to check my six, I saw two MiG-21s closing in fast from my rear quadrant.

"Kevin, keep an eye on those MiGs behind me," I directed.

"Wilco," he replied.

My heart started pounding as I tried to get my plane to turn faster as time slowed down. I had to take the SAM out before the MiGs got any closer; otherwise, I may not have another chance. Still pulling hard on the stick, I fired a radar-seeking missile at the site. "Fox four," I cried out.

A moment later, the site raged in a giant fireball. Then that ominous active radar tone came back. Damn, another site, I thought. How many were there?

"He's got a lock on us," Kevin said. A half-second later he announced," missile in the air."

That was my queue as I dove down through the flak and to the right. It was my only chance to evade the heat-seeking missile and the guns from the MiGs'. The missile resembled a telephone pole as it streaked off my wing and missed me.

Under attack by MiGs, it was standard procedure for us to jettison our ordnance, engage the afterburner, and head for the tree-tops. The Thud could out-race the interceptors down there. My fighter-bomber was no match for the maneuverable MiGs in a dogfight. I knew the MiGs wouldn't follow me through that intense wall of flak. Who in their right mind would?

I checked my right and left side for my wingman Ken Bell, as I dove into the valley again.

"Kev, do you see my wingman?" I asked.

A second passed before Kevin replied, "He's back near our six."

Ken Bell stuck to me like glue throughout the harrowing sequence of events. Later, I discovered that AAA and MiG guns had hit his aircraft. Because of his damaged aileron, Ken could only turn his plane to the right as he followed me down the chute again.

"MiGs are breaking off," Kevin called out.

Smiling, I knew I had made the right decision; although there was no time to rejoice about the MiGs. Surprisingly, we hadn't taken a hit as we came through the flak and set up for another pass.

"Two MiGs to the right," Kevin said anxiously.

I jammed the stick to the right again, decreasing their angle on me. My Thud hesitated and then responded by rolling hard right. I could see the tracers of a 57-millimeter gun from the ground homing in on me. I could do nothing as bullets pelted the bottom of my fuselage and left wingtip.

"We're hit! We're hit!" Kevin yelled.

Glancing outside, I could see metal from the wingtip flapping. Rolling out of the turn, I quickly checked the flight controls and gauges. Everything indicated normal. I couldn't believe it. None of the shells had hit my plane's vital parts. Typically, we'd have to bug out of the fight, but I didn't want to leave that SAM site operational.

I could hear the Strike Force dropping their bombs as they egressed out of the area. I knew all the targets were not destroyed, as there were too many. I knew our fighter bombers would be back tomorrow. Same route, same area. My aircraft was still working well enough to be effective. With the weather clear, I knew we would never have a better chance. I decided to stay until I got that last SAM, or they got me.

I keyed the mic and said. "Strike One, Lincoln 10 flight.

"Go ahead, Lincoln 10," Strike One responded.

"Request permission to stay and take out the last SAM?" I asked.

"Permission granted; rejoin when able," came the reply.

Maneuvering around the flak, I spotted yet another SAM site off the nose of the aircraft. I squeezed off another missile just as the SAMs radar shut down. It didn't matter as the missile already had locked onto the target, blowing the radar sky high.

Smoke and dust from the bombs of the main strike began to drift over the area as Kevin and I strained to spot the original SAM. I lowered the nose of my Thud on the deck for one last look.

At last, I spotted the site through the smoke. I immediately dropped my bombs. The smoke and flak were too thick to get a visual of the damage. Turning my plane a hundred and eighty degrees for one last pass, I hit the site again with my 20-millimeter gun blazing away. The site went up in smoke.

"Lead's off," I replied.

"Two's in trail," came from Ken.

Hearing Ken's voice as we left the industrial complex was reassuring. Mission accomplished. Our two battle-weary Thuds sped toward the tanker and then headed home to base.

Merlyn Hans Dethlefsen was born in Greenville, Iowa, on June 29, 1934. After attending the University of Omaha, he entered the Air Force and began aviation cadet training in 1954.

Captain Dethlefsen served a tour of duty as a fighter pilot in Germany before transferring to a combat squadron in Thailand in October 1966. The 33-year-old officer won the Medal of Honor on his 78th combat mission, precisely one year after Major Fisher earned the first Air Force Medal of Honor of the Vietnam War.

Before finishing his tour in Southeast Asia, Captain Dethlefsen earned the Distinguished Flying Cross and the Air Medal with nine oak leaf clusters.

13

Chapter 2

Major Leo K. Thornsness
F-105 Thunderchief
Medal of Honor

The flak-and-SAM-suppression job of the wild weasel was inherently dangerous. The weasels deliberately flew in range of the North Vietnamese defenses to force the enemy gunners and missile crews to commit themselves. While concentrating on the surface threat, they could never forget about the MiG interceptors lurking nearby. The enemy patiently awaited to sneak in undetected and shoot down an American aircraft with air-to-air missiles or cannon fire.

The wild weasel crews had earned the respect of their comrades. In the north, every vital target was protected by bristling defenses. The weasels constantly took death-defying risks to attack these defenses and defend the main strike force. Relentless is the only way to describe Leo Thorsness.

Thorsness took his aircraft back and forth into the mouth of death during this Medal of Honor sortie. His desire to be the best excelled him in the cockpit and as a prisoner of war.

* * *

On April 19, 1967, four Thuds and I lifted off from Takhli. We were heading for the Xuan Mai Army barracks and storage supply area. The site was located thirty miles to the Southwest of Hanoi. Xuan Mai lay on the edge of the Red River Delta, where rice paddies gave way to forested mountains. We all hoped the defenses around the Army barracks would not be as lethal as those ringing downtown Hanoi.

"Fours off the tanker," said Captain Harold (Harry) E. Johnson. Harry had flown most of his combat missions with me. As my backseater, we were approaching our 100-mission mark. We both were anxious to hit that milestone because it meant a free plane ticket home and an end to our tour in Vietnam.

Everybody at Takhli called me the "old head" weasel pilot. Many Thud pilots at the base never made it to be called an "old head." MiGs chased Harry and me throughout the skies of North Vietnam. We had evaded fifty-three surface-to-air-missiles (SAMs) fired at us to date. Just a couple more missions, and we would be home free.

I did like the flak-and-SAM suppression missions. It was the classical game of chicken. First, we would go in high and let everybody shoot at us. After they fired their missiles, it was our turn. Swooping down, we would pick them off one by one; at least, that was the plan.

Today, we were scheduled to hit the target before the main strike force arrived and hang around after they left to clean up. I always thought it was like trolling for sharks in a canoe.

"Two's in position," called out Tom Madison.

I glanced over and smiled under my oxygen mask. Madison and his backseater Tom Sterling were known throughout the squadron as "Tom and Tom." What are the odds, I wondered? Exiting the tanker, I pushed up the power and turned toward North Vietnam.

We had just crossed the border when Harry said, "Scopes Hot! They're looking for us."

"Let them look," I replied over the rattlesnake tone in my headset. The eerie sound signaled that the enemy missile crews were warming up their SAM radars. They were constantly scanning the skies and trying to get a lock on us.

The rattlesnake whined louder, and Harry's strobes on his scope grew even brighter. "They're closing in on us," Harry announced. Although Harry's warning gear detected the SAM tracking and guidance radars, we had no cockpit indications of an actual launch.

If we were lucky, we'd be able to spot the lethal missile rising from its pad in a cloud of smoke. If not, we would have to resort to desperate maneuvers to avoid the missile if there was time. If our luck ran out, it would be a bad day.

"Three and four go north; two follow me," I instructed over the mic.

"Two . . . Three . . . Four," they all responded.

The two back aircraft peeled off and headed away from Tom and me. Now the North Vietnamese gunners would be forced to divide their attention between us.

"I got a strong signal at one o'clock," Harry stated in a high-pitched voice.

I maneuvered the Thud to the right and locked my piper onto a SAM sit. I hit the pickle button as a radar-seeking Shrike missile flew off the rail into the haze. "Did we get a hit?" I inquired.

"I don't know; I can't see. . . ." Harry replied. "Wait! The signals went off my scope."

That was a good sign, I thought to myself. Most likely, we blew the site up to kingdom come. I rolled to the left, avoiding a line of anti-aircraft fire. Peering through the smoke, I hollered, "Harry, I got a visual on another site straight ahead."

I immediately dove my aircraft down through the curtain of anti-aircraft artillery honing in on us. Selecting the toggle switch to bombs, I hit the pickle button again and dropped a load of cluster bombs dead on the target. Flames burst outward as I pulled out of the steep dive.

"Bullseye," Harry exclaimed gleefully.

Glancing to my right, I could see Tom in close formation as we accelerated toward the treetops. Flying low, near the ground, was our best chance of survival.

"Lead, we're hit," Tom yelled over the radio.

Anti-aircraft rounds found Tom Madison's aircraft. I looked over just in time to see smoke pouring out his only engine.

"Two, you're smoking," I replied.

"Lead, we have an overheat light on—."

"Stay low and head west," I screamed as both the canopies blew off.

"Leo, they ejected," Harry hollered as the two ejection seats arched skyward.

Instantly, the rescue beepers from their parachutes cut through on the radio on the guard channel.

"Leo," Harry screamed over the beeping, "SAM straight ahead."

Diverting my attention forward, I could see the star symbol of the missile site and selected a Shrike. My mind was on my wingman, but I had to get the SAM first. Pressing the firing button, I watched intently as the missile flung off our aircraft and punched directly into the radar.

"Strike three," Harry responded.

"Three and four, say position?" I inquired.

"Ten to the north were in a fight with two MiGs," came the reply.

"Hold on; I'll be there . . ."

"Lead, we're heading home," Three cut in. "My afterburners won't light."

Without the added thrust, I knew he couldn't sustain supersonic speed to outrun the MiG interceptors.

"Lead copies," I responded.

Harry and I were alone as I yanked the Thud around and circled above the descending parachutes.

"Harry, work the rescue craft," I commanded.

Roger. "Crown rescue, we have two downed airmen southeast of the Army barracks," Harry stated over the mic. "Leo, watch out, MiG on our left wing!" he screamed.

In a flash, I picked up the MiG heading straight for the two parachutes. I didn't know if they would shoot at our two pilots while descending helplessly to the ground. I couldn't take the chance.

"Hold on," I said to Harry warning him about the G forces coming.

Reefing the on the stick hard, I rolled to the left and dove toward the ground. At a thousand feet, I leveled off and followed the MiG to the north. Glancing at my airspeed, I saw five hundred and fifty knots. I was driving right up his tailpipe.

I opened up on him with my 20-millimeter at three thousand feet, but I completely missed him. "Crap!" I exclaimed.

I rolled with the MiG, trying to match his every move. I was right in his six when I held the trigger down again and nailed him.

"Leo, look out!" Harry yelled again. "Two MiGs on our tail."

Immediately, I pulled up and hit the afterburners as the MiG in front of me began to leave a trail of smoke. It was good that I didn't get a direct hit, or we would have swallowed some of his debris.

I headed south toward the tanker while leaving the MiGs on my tail in the dust. I had to get gas, or else we would be ejecting too. Both of us followed the progress of the rescue forces on the radio. A prop-driven Sandy directing the on-scene helicopter rescue was already headed toward Tom Madison and Tom Sterling.

With full tanks and only five hundred rounds of ammunition, I left the tanker and flew north again. I keyed the mic and said, "Crown, we got three SAM sites, but there's a lot of anti-aircraft artillery surrounding the barracks."

"Crown rescue copies," the Sandy pilot replied.

"Leo, three MiGs dead ahead passing off our nose," Harry screamed again.

Suddenly, a MiG flew right into my gunsight at two thousand feet off my nose, with pieces falling off his aircraft. I wondered if he was the MiG I had wounded earlier.

"I count three, no four MiGs on our six," Harry's high-pitched voice stated.

I was straining to get my head around.

"I see them. Hold on; I'm going for the treetops." I shoved the throttles as far forward as they would go. The jet lunged ahead as the afterburners kicked into gear. I jinked and jived through the mountain passes, trying to avoid the ground.

"Were okay, were okay. They're breaking off," Harry replied in a lower tone. "But I think they're going after the Sandy."

"Sandy One, you got four MiGs closing in on you," I hollered over the radio. "Keep turning and burning, and you'll be able to outmaneuver them. I'll be there in a minute."

"I got my eye on them," Sandy One responded. "Just get back here fast."

I knew the slow-moving Sandy wouldn't be able to outmaneuver the MiGs for too long. Eventually, even the MiGs would get lucky.

Harry said, "Leo, we're low on fuel again, and we don't have any ammunition."

Looking down at the gauges, I couldn't believe how fast we went through our second tank of gas. "I can't leave Sandy One alone. If we do, he'll be toast."

"Yea, but we don't have any ammo," Harry replied. "How in the hell are we going to help?"

I thought for a second and then said, "I'll get them to chase me." I reefed the stick around and headed back toward the MiGs. I could see them lining up on the small propeller-driven rescue aircraft.

"-105s, high and to the right," Harry yelled.

Thank God, I thought, reinforcements. "Now we got them," I replied, lining up on one of the MiGs. My fellow pilots in the Thuds were a great site to see. For a moment, I thought the tables were turning against us.

"They're bugging out Leo," Harry stated.

Just then, two Thuds launched their missiles at the defensive MiGs.

"Splash one!" "Splash two!" another voice said that I didn't recognize.

I saw flames and billowing smoke from the two MiGs as they crashed near the complex. The Strike force pulverized the Xuan Mai site as smoke rose into the sky. It was a silent testimony of our mission.

"Let's go home," I said softly.

"Fine by me. I've had enough fun for the day," said Harry. "Tanker at 180 degrees at fifty miles."

I turned my aircraft and headed toward the tanker for the third time today. Taking a deep breath, I finally began to relax.

"This is Sandy Two; Sandy One has been shot down over the site."

My mind kicked into gear again. Now both Madison and Sterling were down on the ground with another Sandy.

"Sandy Two, this is Lead," I said. "I'm going to refuel and be back in twenty minutes."

"Negative Lead, the rescue has been called off. It's too hot today." Sandy Two stated.

I knew Madison and Sterling wouldn't have a chance if they stayed overnight in the jungle. But I couldn't return as a single ship; I would be putting Harry and myself in extreme danger, especially with no missiles or ammunition.

"Leo, I don't know where I am?" somebody shouted over the radio. "I got separated from my flight, and I've only got 800 pounds of fuel left."

I didn't recognize the voice, but he knew me. He was probably from my squadron and had flown on my wing before. Either way, a fellow Thud pilot was in trouble and needed help.

"Standby," I replied. "Harry, can you find him on the radar?"

Harry paused and said, "Yea, he's twenty to the north."

"Leo, what should I do?" the shaken Thud voice shouted again.

I had to think of something fast. "Just stay where you are; I'm going to send the tanker north to you," I replied.

"Roger," came the reply.

I felt sorry for the pilot. It wasn't unusual to get lost in battle. Many things could happen in a fight to lose track of your bearings and fuel.

Harry keyed the radio and said, "Tanker One, we need you to head 350 degrees to hook up a buddy low on fuel."

"Tanker One Wilco, watch the screen for MiGs," they asked.

I maneuvered the Thud straight South to the nearest base. Now, we were very low on fuel. Shoving the throttles up, I gradually climbed to get the maximum fuel performance out of the -105.

I heard the lost Thud pilot find the tanker. Amazingly, his aircraft flamed out due to fuel starvation before he got another load of fuel, but got some fuel while gliding down and was able to restart the engines and head home.

"Harry, give me the nearest base; we can't make it back to Takhli?" I said as calmly as I could.

"Keep this heading for Udorn," he replied.

I knew if we could get to the Mekong River, or the fence as we called it, we could coast across the border and into Udorn.

With seventy miles to go, I pulled the power back to idle, and we just glided in. The gauges read empty when the runway appeared just before us. I kept my aimpoint long in case we flamed out in the flare and needed the extra altitude.

As we climbed out of the cockpit, Harry said, "Now that's a full day's work!"

In debrief, I found out the strike had one confirmed kill and that we got four probables. As I expected, Madison and Sterling were captured that night. Who would have known I would join them in the Hanoi Hilton eleven days later?

Leo K. Thorsness was born in Walnut Grove, Minnesota, on February 14, 1932. He enlisted in the Air Force in 1951 and got his wings and a commission in 1954. Completing his education in the service, he graduated from the University of Omaha in 1964 and earned a master's degree from the University of Southern California in 1966.

The veteran airman was an F-105 instructor pilot at Las Vegas, Nevada, before he was assigned to Thailand in October 1966. Eleven days after the Medal of Honor mission, Major Thorsness was shot down over North Vietnam on his 93rd mission, just seven short of the 100 required for a complete combat tour.

After almost six years of captivity, Lieutenant Colonel Leo Thorsness and his backseater, Major Harry Johnson, were released in March 1973. Leo was presented with the Medal of Honor six months later and retired shortly after. During his extraordinary career, he was awarded the Silver Star, the Distinguished Flying Cross with five oak leaf clusters, the Air Medal with nine clusters, and the Purple Heart with one cluster. He shot down one MiG fighter during the Vietnam War.

Chapter 3

Lt. Colonel Joe M. Jackson
C-123 Provider
Medal of Honor

Air Force pilots that flew cargo aircraft to and from isolated Army and Marine camps came under constant siege by the Vietcong. Often risking their lives by flying through areas of hostile ground fire, the transport crews delivered the vital supplies that allowed American soldiers to repel enemy attacks. The big cargo birds could land on a short dirt strip and offload even with engines running. They were also used to carrying the wounded to safety. If the groundfire was so intense that landing was impossible, the crew could airdrop supplies by parachute to the embattled outpost. The cargo ships could also drop Army paratroopers into an objective area for a rapid assault on the elusive enemy.

Imagine being left behind on the ground after a rescue operation. If you're lucky, you'll have Joe Jackson on your side.

* * *

"Joe, are you ready for your flight check today?" the blond-haired Major asked.

I never looked forward to flight evaluations, especially in a combat zone. Flight checks were just something I had to live with as a pilot. Twice a year, the Air Force wanted to be reassured that I still had the skills and knowledge to accomplish the mission effectively and safely, even in Vietnam.

"You bet," I replied. "The question is, are you ready?"

"I'm ready, just let me grab my gear, and I'll meet you at the plane," Major Jesse Campbell, the squadron's flight examiner, responded.

It didn't matter that I was a Lieutenant Colonel and outranked Major Campbell. As an examiner, he had the power to ground me from flying status. I knew he expected a first-rate job from me and would write an objective report on my performance. Checkrides were not something I ever got sweaty palms over, but I also never took them for granted either.

Walking out to my plane, I saw my crew chief, Technical Sergeant Ed Trejo, checking the tires of the C-123. Ed always did a great job with the plane. Rarely did we ever have any maintenance issues.

"Good morning, Colonel," he said cheerfully.

"How are you doing today, Ed?" I asked.

"Great!" Ed chirped. "Did you send your mother a card today?"

Thinking I misunderstood him, I said, "What?"

"Did you send your mother a card?" he said again.

"No, why?" I replied, with a puzzled look on my face.

"It's Mother's Day. Moms always like getting cards on Mother's Day," he smirked.

"Crap, I forgot all about it," I said while kicking my shoe. How could I forget about my Mother? My mom would understand since I was in a combat zone, but it was stupid of me to forget. It was too late now, and I would have to get one when I returned.

"We're ready to go, sir," Staff Sergeant Manson Grubbs said, coming out from underneath the airplane.

"All right, Major Campbell will be in the right seat today for a check-ride on me. Make sure we look sharp," I said.

"Wilco," Ed replied.

Jumping into the left seat, I went through my preflight check, being extra careful not to miss anything. Jesse climbed up the crew hatch five minutes later.

Glancing at Jesse while he strapped into his seat, I said, "The preflight's done, and I'm waiting to get taxi clearance now."

"Great, why don't I get the clearance while you start the engines," he replied.

"Roger," I responded.

Both engines on the Provider started with ease as Ed and Manson buckled up the back end. Taxiing out, I wondered what kind of card I should get for my mom. Did I get her one last year? I couldn't remember. Oh well, I had a check ride to pass first.

Lining up on the runway, I pushed both throttles to the firewall as Aircraft 542 rolled down the strip at Danang Air Base. Lifting off, I yelled, "Gear up."

Jesse reached over and yanked the handle upward, and said, "Gear up."

"Flaps," I stated in unison.

"Flaps up," he replied.

Both of us eased back into our seats as the Provider hummed along. Today's mission was relatively simple if there were any simple missions in Vietnam. We were scheduled to swing north toward the Demilitarized Zone and then back down the coast near Chu Lai, stopping en route to re-supply several outposts.

The weather along the coast was beautiful. We were just about to descend into Chu Lai when the radio erupted.

"Provider 542, this is Ops," crackling over our headsets.

"Ops, this is Provider 542; go ahead," I replied.

"542, we need you back at Danang on the double."

"What's the problem?" I said inquisitively.

There was a long silence, and a man's voice replied, "We have an emergency mission for you. Return to base as soon as possible."

Shrugging my shoulders, I said, "Provider 542, heading back to base."

"That's odd," Jesse responded.

"Yea, something big must have happened," I agreed as I turned the aircraft toward Danang.

After landing and shutting the engines down, I saw my squadron commander walking toward our airplane. I stepped outside to greet him and said, "Hi, boss; what's up?"

"Joe, we have a massive airlift operation underway at Kham Duc. We have to evacuate a thousand troops, and we don't have enough aircraft," he said. "It's a Special Forces camp and has been under siege for three days. The Army just gave the word a few hours ago to evacuate before they get overrun. I need you guys down there as fast as you can turn your plane."

"Give me an hour, and we'll be airborne again," I responded.

"I appreciate it, Joe," he said and walked away.

"No problem," I said, turning to Ed, "Get the fuel truck out here."

"Roger, sir," he replied.

We were airborne again in precisely an hour. This time we were heading in the opposite direction. Kham Duc lay forty-five miles southwest of Danang, near the Laotian border. As we flew inland, the weather began deteriorating.

"Airborne Command post, this is Provider 542; where do you want us?" I asked.

"542, hold south of Kham Duc at nine thousand feet and await further instructions," he replied.

"Provider 542, roger," I said, checking my watch. It was three-thirty in the afternoon.

The evacuation was hectic. The Airborne Command post controlled the flow of cargo planes into Kham Duc. Looking out my side window, I saw the short airstrip lying unprotected on the valley floor. Forward Air Controllers were directing fighter bombers against Vietcong positions surrounding the runway.

Established in a holding pattern, we watched the battle unfold beneath us. Smoke and flames filled the area as exploding ammunition dumps went up in a blaze. Tracers from enemy weapons were visible, even from our altitude.

Listening to the radio, I heard, "Hercules 10, Airborne Command post, understand you have the last guys?"

"Affirmative, they're all out," they responded.

"Well, I guess they didn't need us after all," I told Jesse.

"Nope. Kind of a waste of time," he replied. "Oh well, at least we got your check-ride done."

Curiosity got the best of me as I turned the aircraft toward Danang and asked, "How did I—"

"Command post, there are still three soldiers down there," a high-pitched voice interrupted me.

"What!" the controller replied in amazement.

"This is FAC 23; I can see three combat controllers in a ditch beside the runway."

"Command post copies," the man replied. "Combat controllers, this is Airborne Command post. Do you copy?"

Everyone listening to the radio awaited a response, but there was none.

"Provider 310, can you attempt a landing and pick them up?" Command post asked.

"Provider 310, Wilco," they replied.

Jesse and I watched as Provider 310 made their way to Kham Duc. As -310 approached the runway, flak sprang up from everywhere. The slow-moving cargo ship was like a giant magnet for gunfire.

"Strike 18; I need you to lay down some cluster bombs west of the runway," Command post ordered.

"Strike 18, rolling in now."

"God, those guys are getting hit from every direction," Jesse stated as machine guns and mortars pounded the airstrip.

"I guess the Vietcong were taking their revenge on them," I replied. "Hell, wouldn't you? We just snatched a thousand men out from under their noses."

I watched our sister ship touch down on the dirt strip. Dust flew up from their propellers as they came to a stop.

"Command post, we don't see them," a shaky voice blared out from 310. "We're under intense fire from the edge of the runway. Can you take them out?"

"Negative, not without hitting you, too," they responded.

"We can't stay here any longer," Provider 310 responded as the airplane started to takeoff.

"Damn!" I hollered. "We're going to have to go in," I said as my breathing started to increase.

"I agree," Jesse responded.

As Provider 310 lifted off, the pilot said, "We see 'em. They're in a ditch, crouching two thousand feet down the runway."

"Provider 310, can you make another attempt?" Airborne asked.

"Negative; we're low on fuel and took some hits."

That was all the queue I needed, and I was sure Jesse was reading my mind.

"Provider 542—"

"Roger, we're going in," Jesse said before they could finish their transmission.

There wasn't any question about it; our decision was already made. I couldn't let those three men try and fight their way out; they wouldn't survive.

"I want to come in steep," I said, glaring at Jesse. "The last Provider was too low for too long. I don't want Vietcong taking potshots at me all day."

"I concur," Jesse responded.

Calling on my fighter experience from Korea, I threw the flaps down and pointed the nose a quarter mile before the end of the runway. I knew the Vietcong gunners expected me to follow the exact flight path as Provider 310. I had to devise a new tactic to give us the advantage.

"Airspeed 110 and increasing," Jesse hollered out.

The book said we couldn't fly transports this way, but I figured the guy who wrote the book had never been shot at. I had two problems, the second stemming from the first. I had to avoid reaching 'blow up' speed on my flaps; otherwise, they might return to the neutral position and thus increase our airspeed. Second, if the flaps blew up, I would overshoot the runway. It was a no-win situation.

"Airspeed 125," Jesse yelled nervously.

We were on an elevator ride straight down. It was working; the enemy barely had time to react as we approached the runway. I coaxed the nose up, breaking our dizzying descent just above the treetops, one-quarter a mile from the overrun.

"Stabilizing at 130," Jesse stated while taking a deep breath of relief.

I barely had time to set up a landing attitude as we settled onto the dirt. The runway looked like an obstacle course. A burning helicopter blocked the way just 2,200 feet from the touchdown point. I knew we would have to stop in a hurry.

"Manson, open the cargo door," I yelled over the intercom.

"Opening the cargo door," he replied.

"Reverse thrust," Jesse hollered.

"No!" I yelled back. "If we do, the engines will automatically shut the jets off, and I need them for takeoff. Help me get on the brakes."

We stomped on the brakes like no Indianapolis race car driver ever had, skidding the last two hundred feet. The plane came to rest just before reaching the gutted helicopter. I saw three men scrambling toward our aircraft from the side window.

"Smoke from the left," Jesse screamed, "it's coming from a 122 rocket."

We watched in horror as a shell came to rest just twenty-five feet in front of our noses. Luck was on our side as the deadly projectile was a dud stuck in the center of the runway.

Screaming, I said, "We're getting out of here."

"We got 'em aboard. Go! Go! Go!" Ed yelled from the back.

Easing the throttles up, I taxied around the shell and then rammed the throttles to the stops.

Manson yelled at the top of his lungs, "Incoming."

Immediately an explosion tore up the runway where we had been sitting no more than ten seconds ago.

"They're zeroing in on us," Jesse said. "We'll make it."

The mortar shells followed us down the runway as we picked up speed. Craters dotted the runway as I did my best to dodge them. I saw tracers illuminating a murderous crossfire ahead, but there was no turning back. I would have to fly right through them. It was the first time I was truly scared to death.

We broke ground, slowly picking up speed and climbing toward the intense fire from the far end of the runway. There was nothing I could do but wait and watch. I only wished we could have taken the same elevator ride up as we did coming in.

"Gear!" I yelled.

"Gear coming up," Jesse said with a slight relief in his tone.

After the longest minute of my life, Kham Duc was behind us.

We landed at Danang at five-thirty with our four-man crew and three passengers. After checking our aircraft, miraculously, we didn't even take one hit.

"Well, did I pass my check-ride, Jesse?" I asked with a big smile.

"With flying colors," he said, shaking my hand. "Until next time."

"I hope there won't be a next time like that," I replied.

A man from the back of our plane came up and said, "Hi, sir, my name is Mort Freedman."

Spinning around, I could see the ghostly face of one of the combat controllers we had just rescued.

"I can't tell you how much we appreciate you coming to get us," the Technical Sergeant said as his two buddies joined him.

"Glad to be of service," I said, laughing.

"When we saw the other aircraft take off and leave us, I figured no one would come back for us. We thought we would have to fight it out or be taken prisoners.

"Well, I wasn't going to leave you there," I said reassuringly.

"It's a good thing because we only had eleven magazine clips left between the three of us. But at least we were going to take as many of them as possible."

Turning around, I started to walk back to base operations when Ed yelled, "Colonel, Happy Mother's Day."

Joe M. Jackson was born in Newnan, Georgia, on March 14, 1923. He enlisted in the Army Air Corps in 1941 and sought duty as an aircraft mechanic. After serving as a crew chief in a B-25 bomber unit, Sergeant Jackson began pilot training, earning his wings and a commission in 1943. He flew 107 fighter missions in Korea and won the Distinguished Flying Cross. Colonel Jackson was one of the first Air Force pilots to fly the high-altitude U-2 reconnaissance plane with a solo #42. In the early 1960s, he served on the staff at Strategic Air Command Headquarters and drew up the operations plans for aerial reconnaissance of Cuba during the missile crisis.

After 20 years as a fighter pilot, Colonel Jackson was assigned to transport duty. The 45-year-old officer won the Medal of Honor in Vietnam in 1968 and flew 296 sorties during his combat tour.

Chapter 4

Captain Gerald O. Young

HH-3E Jolly Green

Medal of Honor

The daring pickups by rescue helicopters in hostile territory resulted from the teamwork of a dedicated rescue force. The helicopters and propeller-driven Sandys were airborne within seconds after receiving the scramble order. In the pickup area, the Sandys suppressed the enemy groundfire to protect the downed pilot and the vulnerable choppers.

You are on the second team waiting for your big chance. Then it comes, and you're called into the game. Two rescue choppers before you have been shot down; now it's your turn. How would you react? Here is another extraordinary rescue near the volatile area of Khe Sanh.

* * *

"Rescue 22, return to base," came across the radio.

Puzzled, I responded, "Rescue Center, say again?"

"Rescue 22, we need you back at the base."

I looked at my watch; it read a few minutes past midnight. "Ralph, what do you think?"

"Hell, we're airborne and hot to trot; let's continue," Captain Ralph Brower, my copilot, responded in his aggressive voice.

"It's unanimous, Captain; we're the designated backup," Staff Sergeant Eugene L. Clay added to the conversation.

"Rescue Center, request permission to continue as the backup on this mission?" I replied.

There was a long pause. "Rescue 22, okay, you're cleared to accompany the rescue force, but only as a backup to Rescue 21. Is that understood?"

"Rescue 22 copies," I replied smiling.

I continued flying my Jolly Green helicopter near the back of the rescue armada toward Khe Sanh in northern South Vietnam. We were a hell of a long way from Danang.

"Ralph, find out the latest on the rescue effort at Khe Sanh?" I asked to keep my crew busy.

"Wilco," Ralph said. "Airborne Command post, this is Rescue 22. Say the condition at Khe Sanh?"

After a short pause, Airborne returned with, "A small reconnaissance team is stranded near a cliff and is under heavy fire to the west of the camp. The Vietcong are using the survivors as bait. Earlier, we lost two helicopters attempting to rescue them."

"Rescue 22 copies," Ralph blurted out. "How far back do you want us?"

"Stay at least a couple of miles to the south," replied the controller.

As I approached the site, flares from a C-130 cut through the darkness, illuminating the hillside two miles before us. Low white clouds intensified the bright projectiles.

"All right, I'm going to hold here," I stated.

Suddenly, tracers from the ground erupted.

"Army 10 and 11, you're cleared in," the controller directed.

"Here we go," Ralph said as we watched the two Army gunships roll in on their targets.

The two choppers reacted swiftly, evading a withering fire of bullets, and answered with a stream of air-launched rockets. Glancing outside, I could see the primary rescue ship, Rescue 21, hovering a half mile to my right.

Then the ground fire ceased as suddenly as it had started.

"Rescue 21, your path is clear," the airborne controller said. "Proceed to the pickup point."

"Rescue 21, rolling," they responded.

The primary Jolly slowly started moving from their position along the hillside, settling at the base next to a steep cliff. As soon as the chopper set down, gunfire erupted from atop the hillside, sending artillery down upon them.

"Their paths are not clear," Ralph said in a trance." "The North Vietnamese are right on top of them."

"God, their sitting ducks," I replied, watching sparks fly off the Jolly as bullets pelted their machine.

Rescue 21 was not on the ground for more than ten seconds before they started moving out from the murderous barrage.

"Rescue 21 has three survivors aboard," the shaky voice said. "There's two more down there, but they can't get to us. We're also leaking fuel and oil."

We both watched the primary rescue bird as smoke and flames followed its movements.

Ralph said, "Rescue 21, you'll never make Danang. Head zero-nine-zero to the strip at Khe Sanh."

"Roger, Rescue 21 copies. The landing zone is too hot at this time. Recommend we abort the mission?" they responded.

"Abort my ass," I said over the intercom. "We came here to do a mission. What do you guys say?"

"Hell, that's why we volunteered as the backup Captain," Ralph replied.

Sergeant Clay also responded, "Me too; let's get those last two out."

"Command post, Rescue 22 is going in," I said forcefully.

"Rescue 22, we don't—"

"-22's inbound," I screamed back. "Ralph, you direct the support fire from the Army gunships; I'll maneuver into position."

"Roger," he responded, tightening the straps on his seat,

"Army 10 and 11, can you take out the guns near the top of the hill above the survivors?" Ralph asked.

"Wilco," came the response, "coming around again."

I weaved the giant helicopter around the valley floor. "Sergeant Maysey, get ready. I want you to jump out as soon as I touchdown and get those last two. Clay, you stay on board and tuck them in. Be sharp; it's got to be a team effort if we're going to make this one."

"Roger, Captain," both men responded in unison.

It took all my energy to maneuver the helicopter along the valley floor in the darkness. Night rescues were just plain nasty; I reminded myself as we approached the cliff. As I rounded the last corner, the black sky lit up from the enemy firing at me. Then the Army gunships started strafing the hillside.

"Hold on, it's going to get hairy," I said, easing the chopper down a the base of the cliff.

"Watch your rotor and the trees," Ralph cried out.

"I got it," I replied as I set one wheel down on the ground while the other was dangling over the side of the cliff.

"Maysey, take off," I yelled.

Out the side window, I could see Sergeant Maysey running into the forest as Sergeant Clay spun up our machine gun.

I was hanging in suspended animation, awaiting Maysey and the survivors. Instantly, I could hear, "ping. . . . ping. . . . ping." as the enemy was homing in on my position.

A minute later, Sergeant Clay hollered, "Everybody's aboard let's get out of here."

I saw dark stick figures moving in the woods as I applied full power and started raising the collective.

Suddenly, a rifle-launched hand grenade exploded above us. *Kaboom!*" came from the engine compartment as the chopper began shaking in my hands.

"Were hit!" Ralph screamed. "Engine oil pressure is gone."

Sparks flew out from the side as I fought with all my might to hold the craft steady. It was no use; I could feel it slipping away.

"Hold on; we're going down," I announced.

Immediately, the Jolly Green hit the ground and started cascading end over end down the hill. Flames flew out from every direction.

After two flips, the chopper stopped on the side of the hill. Fire engulfed the cockpit as we were hanging upside down. My clothes began to catch on fire.

With one swift kick, I knocked out my side window and released my seat belt. I thought whatever lay ahead of me was better than burning to death. Falling out through the window, I rolled and tumbled a hundred yards to the bottom of the hill.

Incredible, the flames followed me. Frantically I beat them out with my gloved hands, but not before the heat scorched my legs.

An eternity passed before I looked up and saw the chopper on fire above me. Then I heard moaning sounds to my left.

"Ralph?" I said softly.

Crawling over to the man, I realized he was one of the survivors I had picked up. Having been thrown clear of the wreckage, he lay semi-unconscious with his boot on fire. Using my hands, I smothered the flames out.

Then my mind went to Ralph and the rest of my crew, still trapped in the mangled helicopter above. I tried hysterically to crawl up the side of the hill. As I got close to the helicopter, the flames and heat became too intense, forcing me back down the mountain. I tried again, but the enemy was peering over the side this time and began firing at me.

Realizing I couldn't reach the chopper, I dragged the survivor into thick bushes. Propping his head up, I started to treat him for shock. I also tried to conceal him with anything I could find.

I sat and waited for another rescue chopper to come, but it didn't.

Two hours later, a pair of A-1E Sandys arrived overhead.

Grabbing my radio, I turned it on. Instantly, the emergency beeping sound from our aircraft was on every channel.

"Can anybody hear this is Rescue 22?" I said over the radio.

No one answered. I didn't expect them to since the emergency signal was overriding my radio transmission.

I watched the Sandys circle above, and then they left the area. My heart sank to the bottom of my stomach. I knew it was too dangerous for them to try another rescue at night.

Lying in the bushes, I waited for the sun to rise over the hillside while my chopper continued burning.

As the eastern sky lightened, the roar from the Sandys brought me out of a daze. Emerging from the bushes, I turned on my radio again. The emergency beeper was still going off, clogging up all the radio channels. Grabbing an orange flare out of my emergency pack, I ignited it. The signaling device sent a plume of bright red smoke down the hillside.

A Sandy passed overhead, rocking his wings as I pointed to the man in the bushes. My spirits increased as I was able to let them know our location.

Suddenly, I spotted movement above as the enemy was crouching down. They were using me as bait to lure another chopper into the area. Waiting patiently, they didn't fire on Sandy for fear of giving up their position.

I wanted to warn the Sandys, but without the use of the radio, I couldn't. They left as I was about to wave them off with my hands.

In the distance, I could hear the whooshing sound of a helicopter on the other side of the hill. They had to be picking up the other survivors. A minute later, the sound disappeared as the helicopter took off.

At first, I thought the rescue force had forgotten about me, but two more Sandys returned a few hours later. Circling overhead, I knew my rescue was imminent.

Immediately, one of the Sandys laid down a smokescreen between the enemy and me. The other fired his rockets into the North

Vietnamese, entrenched on the side of the hill. From the opposite direction, two helicopters came barreling along the valley floor.

Within seconds, the North Vietnamese ran around the smokescreen and started firing from the south. As one Sandy made a low pass, the enemy scored a direct hit, ripping the A-1E with armor-piercing shells. Smoke poured out from his engine as he departed the area.

The other A-1E zoomed in from a different direction and laid down another smokescreen to shield me and protect the rescue helicopters.

The rescue was not working. The North Vietnamese was still firing through the smoke, making the pickup dangerous. I had to do something fast; otherwise, we would be captured.

Running over to the survivor, I said, "Listen, buddy, I have to leave you here."

His eyes were open, but I wasn't sure if he understood what I was saying. "If you understand me, blink once." He blinked.

"I need to lead the enemy out of this area so the rescue force can come in and get you. This area is just too hot."

Without waiting for a response, I threw more underbrush on him to cover as much of his body as possible.

Heading down the embankment, I could hear and see the enemy making their way after me. They pursued me throughout the day as I ran through the trees as fast as my legs would take me.

Soon I made it into an open field surrounded by tall elephant grass. I knew the enemy was trailing me by a half-mile. They wanted to see if I would contact the rescue force. I decided to wait until I was further away. I didn't want to expose the rescue force to an ambush.

Running through the day, I finally stopped at the edge of a hill and waited to see if the enemy was still following me. After a few hours without movement, I turned on my radio. I was ecstatic to find the emergency beacon was no longer beeping.

I called, "Rescue forces, this is Rescue 22, do you copy?"

"Rescue 22, we have you loud and clear, say position," a Sandy pilot replied.

"Rescue 22 is six miles west of my original position near an open field," I answered.

"Rescue 22, we're on our way," they said.

A helicopter immediately arrived and picked me up, seventeen hours after our crash.

I jumped onto the helicopter and asked, "Did you get the guy I left in the underbrush?"

"Yes sir, we did," one of the pararescue men said. "While the North Vietnamese were following you through the elephant grass, we went in and got him."

"Thank goodness," I replied as I sat back and relaxed for the ride back to Danang. My ordeal was finally over.

Gerald O. Young was born in Chicago on May 19, 1930. Before entering Air Force aviation cadet training, he served as a Navy enlisted man. Lieutenant Young won his wings and a commission in 1958. Captain Young reported for rescue helicopter duty in Vietnam in 1967. The 37-year-old pilot won the Medal of Honor on his 60th combat mission.

CHAPTER 5

1st Lieutenant James P. Fleming
UH-1 Huey
Medal of Honor

In the ideal situation, the rescue helicopter could locate the downed airman quickly by homing in on their emergency locator beacon. Contacting the Sandys on their survival radio, the survivor would authenticate his identity. This would prevent an English-speaking North Vietnamese from using the emergency frequency to lure American aircraft into a flak trap.

Today James Fleming speaks to many young officers in the military. He provides them with accounts of his action in Vietnam and insight into being a leader in today's Air Force. He is a compelling speaker with a gripping message.

* * *

"Mayday! Mayday! Mayday! This is SF-2; we need fire support now," splattered the airways.

"Paul, where's that coming from?" I asked impatiently.

"I don't know, but it's from a Special Forces Green Beret Unit," he responded.

"They must be close for us to pick up their transmission this low," I replied, scanning our fuel situation. Half tanks was enough gas for two hours of flight.

I watched my copilot, Major Paul McClellan, hurriedly flip through our flight book, trying to find the location of SF-2.

"Any lu—" I started to say.

"SF-2, this is Spider 19 overhead," a familiar voice piped in.

"Is that Major Anonsen flying FAC today?" I asked.

Paul replied, "Sure is."

"Spider 19, we're being overrun," the panicked lieutenant screamed. "I repeat, we need evacuation now."

"Spider 19, this is Tiger 11, say position?" I cried, overriding their transmission.

"Tiger 11, I'm twenty clicks west of Duc Co near the river," Spider 19 responded.

" Turning to Paul I asked, "How far are we away?"

"Not more than ten miles," Paul said, using his fingers to measure the distance on the map.

That was all I needed to know. "Spider 19, Tiger 11 is headed your direction."

"Get ready in the back, boys; we're going in," Paul said over the intercom.

"Locked and loaded, sir," Staff Sergeant Fred Cook yelled, cocking his M-60.

Gyrating my Huey back and forth, I followed the terrain across the western highlands of South Vietnam.

"Spider 19, how many for the recovery?" I inquired.

"I'm guessing about six, Jim," recognizing who I was. "They're under intense fire from heavy machine guns to the south. BREAK! SF-2, can you make the clearing one hundred yards to the west?"

"Negative, were pinned down and can't move," as gunfire intertwined with the lieutenant's transmission. "We need help now!"

"Tiger 12 is on station," I yelled as we arrived on scene.

"Damn!" I hollered, approaching the river. "Major Eppinger beat us to the punch."

Disgusted and shaking his head, Paul said, "Looks like our sister ship did it again."

Sighing, I replied, "We'll stay back in case they need us."

"Tiger 12, your primary," Major Anonsen from FAC directed.

Eppinger replied, "Tiger 12 copies.

Two miles north of SF-2, I pulled up to a thousand feet and hovered in a static position. I spotted the forward air controller, doing figure eights around SF-2s position. Our sister ship, Tiger 12; positioned itself just north of the Green Berets.

"SF-2, can you pop a smoke?" Anonsen asked.

"Wilco," cried the lieutenant.

A second later red smoke filtered through the dense foliage, pinpointing their position.

Suddenly, the hillside became a shooting gallery as the enemy also pinpointed the Special Forces unit. Heavy machine gun fire sprayed the trapped Americans two hundred yards to the south.

"Fireball flight," Major Anonsen yelled, "are you up?"

"Fireball flight of two is inbound, three to the north," they replied.

"Roger, I need you to take out the big guns to the south," Anonsen directed.

"Sierra Hotel," the gunship pilot replied. "We're starting our attack run now."

Paul and I watched nervously as the two gunships rolled in from the river toward the enemy. Each craft sent streams of fire slanting down into the jungle, ripping the enemy positions with high explosive rockets and machine gun fire. The enemy instantly answered back.

Smoke and tracers flew in all directions as I watched intently.

"The second gunship took a hit," Paul said.

Finding the gunship against the jungle floor, I saw small puffs of smoke trailing the craft.

"He's going back in again," I said.

"He's crazy," Paul replied.

The smoking gunship fired more rockets into the enemy and set up for yet another pass. On his third flyover, a large projectile nailed his engine as flames projected outward from the top of his helicopter.

"Fireball 2 is hit!" came the expected cry.

"He's in some serious trouble," I said as the crippled ship pulled out of the battle.

"Tiger 12, can you get close to the gunship?" Anonsen queried.

"Affirmative, we're on our way," I responded.

We headed north across the river as the crippled chopper began to autorotate. Tiger 12 maneuvered in position closely behind them.

As the gunship landed hard on the sandy bank, Tiger 12 wheeled into the north a few hundred feet away. The crew spilled out of the burning helicopter and jumped aboard Tiger 12.

"Tiger 12 has all the crew and is heading for Duc Co," they called out.

"Roger—12. BREAK. Tiger 11, you're primary now."

"-11 copies," I said, gripping the controls even tighter.

"SF-2, I need you at the clearing to the west for pickup," Major Anonsen directed.

"Roger, we're on the move," the lieutenant replied as the enemy guns subsided in the background.

"Tiger 11, do you have the Landing Zone (LZ) in site?"

"Affirmative," I said, dumping my nose and descending toward the clearing.

"Fireball 1, I'll need a couple more passes to the south," Anonsen yelled.

The gunship circled in from the west and began strafing the area with his guns, forcing the enemy gunners to keep their heads down as I approached the LZ.

At treetop height, I screamed, "Paul, are we clear on your side?"

"Negative, we can't fit between the trees," he replied, "our rotor won't clear."

I took a deep breath and said, "All right, we need to find another spot."

"How about along the river bank?" Paul asked.

Calculating the risk, I said, "Can't be any worse than this," as I moved the collective forward, "Spider 19, we can't make the primary LZ. We're moving to the river."

"Spider copies," he responded. "SF-12, retrograde back to the river."

Over the river, I did a teardrop maneuver and swung my tail boom over the water. The skids bumped lightly on the sandy bank.

"Sergeant Cook, do you see them?" I cried out.

Searching frantically out the door, he replied, "Negative, sir, they're nowhere in sight."

More gunfire erupted. This time from all directions as we took several minor hits in the fuselage.

"SF-2 can you make it to our position," I yelled over the radio.

A garbled voice followed. "SF-2. . . ."

"What did he say?" I asked Paul.

Paul responded, "I couldn't catch what he was saying either."

"This is SF-2 . . . " rat . . . tat . . . tat . . . "can't make the pickup." "Crap, we're a sitting target here," I screamed. "We have to get out of here."

Paul turned his head and hollered, "Cookie and Johnson, let 'em have it."

I backed the chopper up and across the riverbank as, the two gunners let loose with a pair of M-60s. Firing hundreds of rounds per second in all directions, they raked the North Vietnamese emplacements.

We moved northbound, away from the crossfire as my heartbeat started to slow down. "That was close," I said as my hands shook on the collective.

"Too close," Paul added, "and to top that off, we're getting low on fuel."

Turning the chopper around to survey the area we had just transited, I said, "If we withdraw now, they'll get killed."

"This is SF-2; we've made it to the river," the lieutenant yelled. "We've ringed our position with Claymores. Come get us!"

"Get ready; we're going in again," I said, glancing out my left window. The other gunship was still smoking along the other riverbank. The site of the downed chopper made me realize I might be next. I was scared to death as I returned for the second time.

I selected a spot just north of my original one, but I couldn't put my skids on the beach this time. Lowering the helicopter, I ducked below a high bank to partially shield us from the continuing deadly barrage. It was no use. The North Vietnamese knew precisely where I was as bullets ripped into our ship.

"Johnson, throw out the rope ladder," I commanded.

"Already did," he replied without breaking stride in firing his M-60.

Suddenly, a Claymore went off as pieces of a North Vietnamese soldier flew through the air.

"Jesus! Did you see that?" I asked.

Paul said, "Yea, nailed one, at least."

A Green Beret troop finally popped over the top with his back to us, firing his gun simultaneously. Then five more of our troops came dashing over the hill as they fired toward the west.

"Cookie, they're coming in on your side!" I hollered.

"Crap!" Sergeant Johnson yelled from the other side. "My gun is jammed."

I thought to myself, this was going to be close. Too damn close for comfort.

As the Green Berets made their way to the door, Sergeant Cook continued firing with one hand while hoisting the soldiers aboard with the other. I was amazed at my five foot seven, one hundred and twenty pound gunner lifting the two hundred pound Special Forces boys into the back end.

I struggled to hold the craft steady while it rocked back and forth with the added weight of the additional bodies. "Cookie, holler when you have the last one," I said impatiently.

"Two to go," he said, throwing another one in the back of the helicopter.

From my left side, I could see Fireball 1 rolling in. His nose was pointing directly at me. I knew the enemy was on the other side of the bank. They would have an easy thirty-foot shot down on us if they reached the top.

Smoke poured from Fireball 1's guns as he strafed within twenty yards of our position.

Suddenly my windshield cracked from a bullet, leaving a hole the size of a silver dollar. Then another splintered the glass. "Coo—"

"Go! Go! Go!"

Without waiting anymore, I swung the chopper to the left and added full power speeding down the river. Frustrated, the enemy continued to fire on us until we were well down the river.

I immediately headed for Duc Co since I was low on fuel and didn't know the status of the crew I had just picked up.

"Lieutenant!" a man said over my shoulder. Turning around, I could see a bloody soldier.

"Yea," I replied.

"My name's Randolph Harrison," he said, catching his breath. "Thanks for saving our lives."

"Don't think anything about it," I replied, smiling. "That's what the four of us get paid to do."

James P. Fleming was born in Sedalia, Missouri, on March 12, 1943. He was commissioned through the Reserve Officer Training Corps program upon graduation from Washington State University in 1966.

First Lieutenant Fleming was assigned to helicopter duty in Vietnam in July 1968. The 25-year-old had been an Air Force pilot for less than two years when he won the Medal of Honor. Before completing his Southeast Asia tour in May 1969, Lieutenant Fleming flew 810 helicopter sorties in combat.

In addition to the Medal of Honor, he earned the Silver Star, the Distinguished Flying Cross, and the Air Medal with seven oak leaf clusters.

CHAPTER 6

Major Bernard F. Fisher
A-1E Skyraider
Medal of Honor

Often the airman in Vietnam were more concerned with saving lives than taking them. President Lyndon B. Johnson made the following remarks at Major Fisher's presentation ceremony: "I should like to point out that his desire to save lives instead of taking lives is not just confined to Major Fisher. It is rather, I think, typical of all our men in Vietnam. It is particularly true of those who served with Major Fisher in the most brutal air war in the history of the United States. Like Major Fisher, all of these airmen have accepted an additional risk. These men are conducting the most careful and self-limited air war in history. They are trying to apply the maximum amount of pressure with the minimum amount of danger to our people." Major Fisher was the first Air Force member to receive the Medal of Honor in Vietnam.

* * *

The flight briefing room became quiet as I approached the podium. Glancing at the five pilots before me, I knew they wouldn't be happy with today's mission.

"Guys were going back into "the tube" at A Shau Valley," I stated.

I could see their disappointment before I finished the sentence. Their long, drawn-out faces said it all. Nobody in his right mind wanted to fly in the A Shau Valley.

"Oh, you're kidding me," Captain Jon Lucas said with a sour face.

"And to make it worse," Captain Dennis Hague added, "the weather is supposed to be less than a thousand feet."

"The tube" played host to one of our Special Forces camps. Less than a mile wide and six miles long, it provided little maneuvering room for bombing and strafing runs against the enemy. Bad weather made flying in the tube almost impossible.

The A Shau Valley was located hundred and fifty miles north of Pleiku Air Base, near the Laotian border. The Special Forces camp, with twenty American troops and 275 South Vietnamese soldiers, had been attacked by over 2,000 North Vietnamese Army Regulars. The siege was on its second day, and the defenders had been forced into a single bunker in the northern corner of the outpost. The defenders were depending on our airstrikes to slow the enemy's advance.

"I'll take the lead, and Paco, you take number two off my wing," I said.

"Roger," Captain Francisco "Paco" Vazquez replied.

Major Dafford W. "Jump," Myers motioned with his hand, "What kind of defenses are we looking at today?"

I shook my head and said, "The valley floor is ringed with over 20 anti-aircraft artillery pieces and hundreds of automatic weapons."

"Anybody else have any questions?" I asked.

All the pilots shook their heads. Everybody was afraid to ask questions because the answers were too depressing. It was just one of those things we had to do.

"Okay, my call sign is Hobo 51," I said, looking at the flight authorization sheet. "Paco, you take 52. Jump, yours is Surf 41, and the rest of you already have yours."

"All right, I'll meet you at the airplanes," I said as I folded up my briefing guide.

Thirty minutes later, I signaled to start our engines in unison. After getting takeoff clearance, we taxied out to the runway. Low-lying clouds were slowly invading the central highlands around Pleiku. Soon, we arrived over the target to find a cloud deck hanging over the valley.

"Hobo 51, there is no way we can get below these clouds," Jump said over the radio.

Scanning the area, I said, "Try finding a hole we can punch through."

"Hobo 51, this is Airborne Command post," the controller said. "The airstrip is under heavy fire. Can you give us some assistance?"

"Command post, we're having trouble getting below this deck," I replied. Searching through the murk, I finally found a small hole in the undercast near the valley's north end. "Hobo and Surf flight, follow me; I found a way in."

"We're with you," Paco responded.

"Surf 43 and 44, stay on top, and watch for MiGs," I directed as I banked up my Skyraider and headed for the hole.

"Surf 43 and 44 copies," came over the radio.

I knew Lucas and Hague would not be happy patrolling the skies above the valley while we were having all the fun down below, but I didn't want to take everybody into no man's land before I knew what was waiting for us.

At eight hundred feet, we broke out above the trees to find the ragged cloud ceiling obscuring the tops of the surrounding hills. This forced us to operate at low altitudes, constantly in the sights of the enemy gunners.

"Hobo and Surf flight, it's going to be tight, so stay close," I said. "We'll have to attack from the north and then turn around and come back out this direction."

I knew the North Vietnamese would fill the approach to the valley with a deadly curtain of groundfire.

"Hobo 51, this is Platoon 22 on the ground," the American voice said. "Your main concentration of enemy gunners is along the valley's south wall."

"Hobo 51, we're starting our attack run now," I replied, gripping the stick tighter.

On our first run, each of us popped off a bomb in the direction of the main enemy ground forces. Instantly, the enemy gunners accurately found us in their sights.

"Surf 42's hit," Captain Huber King yelled.

"How bad," I questioned.

"They blew my canopy off, and I can't see anything out in front of me," he replied.

Banking my aircraft around a hundred and eighty degrees to get back to the other side of the valley, I said, "Surf 42, head home. You can't do anymore today."

Immediately, Captain King pulled up through the clouds and returned to Pleiku.

As we returned to the tube's northern part, the deadly flak came from all directions. It was like flying inside Yankee Stadium with the fans firing machine guns at us.

Racing out of the canyon, it was just Paco, Jump, and I now. Catching my breath, I yelled, "All right, let's hit them again."

Hurtling our aircraft back into the valley, I kept the formation just below the scud deck, weaving along the mountain edges.

Just before launching my rockets, I noticed smoke pouring from Jump's aircraft.

"Surf 41, you're hit," I screamed.

His machine lurched back and forth before Jump could reply, "I took something big in the engine compartment."

Instantly, I could tell his engine was having significant problems as it coughed out smoke, and bright orange flames appeared.

"Jump, you're on fire and burning clear back past your tail," I yelled. Within ten seconds, his propeller stopped cold.

Coasting along, Jump was too low to bail out, eliminating one of his options. "Hobo 51," he said in a high-pitched voice, "I'm going to have to put it down on the airstrip below."

"Roger," I said, knowing it was the only thing he could do. This wasn't going to be a walk in the park, I thought to myself. The enemy controlled the area surrounding the airstrip and was flanked by heavy guns.

Jump began a wide gliding turn toward the runway. "Hobo 51, you'll have to guide me down; I can't see."

"Wilco, turn left and start your descent now," I said.

"Rog."

Watching him intently I said, "Surf 41, stop turn, and slow it down; you're going too fast."

"I'm trying," Jump responded.

"Can you release your belly tank?" I asked.

"Negative, it won't release," he replied back.

I watched Jump cross the landing threshold, still going too fast. If he didn't slow down, he would crash into the trees at the end of the runway.

"Raise your gear! Raise your gear!" I screamed over the radio.

Jump retracted the wheels just before the aircraft settled onto the steel planks. Sparks flew as his belly tank blew, sending skyward a massive fireball of flames. The deadly fire made a path following him as he skidded several hundred feet before spilling off to the right side of the runway.

"Jump, get out of there!" I hollered.

There was no response as his A-1E turned into a giant fireball. I waited and watched as my worst nightmare came true. My good friend wasn't going to make it.

"Command post, I have a man down," I yelled. "Send a rescue craft ASAP."

"Hobo 51, we're working with rescue now," they replied.

I continued my left turn on the east side of the airstrip while smoke poured out of Jump's aircraft. Then suddenly, he came out from the right side of the cockpit. Running on the top edge of his wing, he jumped to the ground and scrambled off into some brush, away from the enemy.

I circled the airstrip, oblivious to the enemy firing at me.

"Command post, the downed airman is on the right side of the runway, and he's probably hurt," I informed them. I could see Jump waving at me as I passed overhead, but I had no idea about his injuries.

"Hobo 51, a rescue helicopter is twenty minutes away," Command post stated.

Twenty minutes, that was too long, I told myself. He would never survive.

I needed reinforcements now as I said, "Surf 53 and 54, get down here. I need some help."

"We're on our way," Lucas replied excitedly.

Suddenly, the enemy began making their way across the runway toward Jump. I open fired on them with all my guns as they turned and began retreating.

After several strafing runs, Command post returned and said, "Hobo 51, the rescue chopper is still twenty minutes away."

Furious, I yelled, "What the hell's going on up there?"

"Hobo 51, I have another chopper above the overcast, but they can't find a hole," he replied. "Can you escort them through the clouds?"

"Negative, I can't leave," I screamed impatiently. "If I do, they'll get him."

"Hobo 51, say intentions," Command post inquired.

I had to make a quick decision. There wasn't any time to wait for a rescue. "Command post, I'm going in to pick him up."

"Hobo 51, we advise you not to; it's too dangerous," they replied.

I knew my plan wasn't wise, but all my options were exhausted. I had to get Jump out of there because he was family.

"Command post, I'm going to land. Paco, protect my left side," I screamed.

"Hobo 52, copies," Paco replied.

Setting up for my approach, I could barely see the runway through the blowing smoke. I kept my power up since I couldn't tell what obstructed the runway. At the last moment, I saw the tiny airstrip and landed long. The runway was littered with debris everywhere. Dodging and weaving, I just missed a garbage can and a large tin roof blown over from the main camp.

Approaching the end of the runway, I realized I was too fast to stop safely. With no time to spare, I slammed the throttle forward and took back off.

"Command post, I didn't make it," I screamed. "I'm going to try it again."

"Hobo 51, hurry up," Paco said. "They're moving in closer."

Yanking my aircraft around in a tight hundred-and-eighty-degree turn, I set up to land from the opposite direction. Enemy gunfire pelted my plane as I completed the maneuver in less than a hundred feet.

This time, I touched down at the end of the runway. I hit the brakes as hard as I could. Screaming down the 2,500-foot strip, I raised the flaps up to put more weight on the brakes. The aircraft started to skid on the damp steel planking.

A few seconds later, I watched the last of the steel planks go underneath the nose of my aircraft as I continued skidding off the end. Out of the corner of my eye, I could see a bunch of 55-gallon drums sitting out in the weeds with my airplane heading directly for them. I cringed waiting for the impact as my plane stopped within a few feet of the first drum. My heart was pounding through my chest.

Jamming the rudder in, I turned the plane around as my tail brushed against one of the drums.

Pushing the power up, I taxied back through the obstacle course, trying to find Jump. Suddenly, he popped out from behind the brush, waving both arms vigorously. I slammed on the brakes again as my Skyraider slid a hundred feet past him.

Immediately, fire erupted from my left side. The enemy finally figured out what was happening and was now targeting me. Within a second, Paco and Lucas doused the area with their rockets.

Opening the canopy, I stood in the seat, expecting to see Jump. He was nowhere in sight.

"Damn!" I yelled to myself. He must be hurt worse than I thought. Reaching down in the cockpit, I set the parking brake and climbed onto the right seat.

I was about to leave the cockpit when I saw two red beady eyes trying to crawl up the back of my wing.

"Jump, hold on, I'll get ya," I yelled over the engine noise.

Leaning over the right seat, I grabbed Jump by the seat of his pants and pulled him head-first onto the cockpit floor. His head made a gut-wrenching crack as he collided with the floor.

Smiling, Jump said, "Sorry I couldn't get here faster; I was running as fast as my forty-six-year-old legs would go."

Barely listening, I released the brakes and jammed the throttle to the wall. Accelerating, I maneuvered the Skyraider around the shell craters and debris while the North Vietnamese concentrated their fire on us.

At minimum takeoff speed, I pulled back on the stick just as my three wingmen made another pass, pulverizing the enemy.

"Command post, Hobo 51 is airborne," I responded.

"Roger Hobo 51, you're cleared to return to base," Command post replied.

"Hobo and Surf flights rejoin on me," I directed.

As I pulled through the clouds and out of the A Shau Valley for the last time, Paco, Lucas, and Hague closed in on my position. Smoke poured from Lucas's aircraft as we headed home. All four of us were out of ammunition.

After we landed, I counted nineteen hits from hostile gunfire in my Skyraider, but more importantly, I had my good friend Jump with me.

DONALD PICKINPAUGH

Born in 1927, Bernard F. Fisher served briefly in the Navy at the end of World War II and in the Air National Guard from 1947 to 1950. The Idaho native began Air Force officer training in 1951.

Before his assignment to Vietnam, he spent his entire Air Force career as a jet fighter pilot in the Air Defense Command. While stationed at Homestead Air Force Base, Florida, Major Fisher was recognized twice due to his landing F-104 Starfighters after a complete failure of the engine oil system. He saved the crippled craft on each occasion when ejection would have been the safest course of action.

In 1965 Bernie Fisher volunteered for duty in Vietnam and traded his fast-moving jet for the venerable Skyraider. As a 1st Air Commando Squadron member, he flew 200 combat sorties from July 1965 to June 1966. In addition to the Medal of Honor, Major Fisher earned the Silver Star, the Distinguished Flying Cross, and the Air Medal with six oak leaf clusters.

CHAPTER 7

Captain Steven L. Bennett
OV-10 Bronco
Medal of Honor

The forward air controller flies low and slow over his target. They mark it with smoke grenades or rockets, and call in the strike aircraft. They would remain near the target, working with the tactical pilots so bombs and other weapons were delivered with maximum precision. Often the opposing forces were separated only by a few meters in the jungle undergrowth. The utmost accuracy was required to ensure the safety of friendly soldiers.

After the attack, the forward air controller would fly in to check battle damage and determine if the target was destroyed or if more firepower was needed.

Steve Bennett was the last Air Force member in Vietnam to receive the Medal of Honor. The Forward Air Controller (FAC) drove his aircraft into a line of fire five straight times. In the end, he gave his life for a South Vietnamese platoon.

* * *

"Hey Jar-head, you ready to take off?" I yelled jokingly.

Captain Mike Brown finished checking the oil and swung around and said, "You're just jealous you're not a Marine."

"Jealous! Jealous of what?" I asked, egging him on.

"That you can't be the few, the proud, the Marines," he said, chuckling.

"Yeah, right," I replied. "We'll come aboard, and let me show you what the few, the proud, and the Air Force do for a living."

"I'm ready. Oil looks good in both engines, and she's full of ammo," he replied.

"All right then, let's head up to Quang Tri and kick some butt."

I enjoyed flying with Mike as my backseater. We had been flying together for two months, roaming the skies over South Vietnam in my OV-10.

At first, I thought Mike was crazy for volunteering for duty in Vietnam. As a Company commander stationed in Hawaii, he was able to finagle a tour with my squadron to assist us in directing naval gunfire.

This afternoon sun began beating down on us as we completed our preflight. Danang was an oven in the summertime. For that matter, the entire country of South Vietnam was hotter than hell, and the war didn't cool things off.

Thirty minutes later, we were airborne, heading northwest along the coast.

"Command post, Wolfman 45, is with you south of Quang Tri," I said checking in.

"Wolfman 45, proceed to Quang Tri and circle overhead," the man replied.

"Roger -45 out," I said, descending into the valley at Quang Tri. As I maneuvered inbound, low clouds began forming north of the valley.

"Newport News, Wolfman 45 is primary," Mike said over the radio.

"Newport copies. We'll commence firing in one minute," the heavy cruiser replied.

From the Gulf of Tonkin, USS Newport News and R.B. Anderson began firing into enemy positions at Quang Tri.

Circling south of the target area, we watched anxiously as the first volley roared in.

"Newport, adjust range two-zero-zero meters north," Mike directed while checking the hits through his binoculars.

"Copy two-zero-zero north," they replied.

For the next two hours, I flew in circles while Mike radioed instructions to the heavy cruiser allowing the ship to pinpoint their fire against enemy positions.

"Wolfman 45, this is Command post."

"Go ahead," I said.

"Wolfman 45, your relief is delayed on the ground in Danang for an hour and a half. Request you remain on station until then?"

Looking at my fuel, I said, "Command post, no problem, we can stay."

"Thanks for the help; we appreciate it," they replied.

As darkness set in, Mike continued spotting targets for the Navy guns. I kept circling, staying far away.

"Wolfman 45, Tonco 64 flight is inbound. Where do you want our ordinance dropped?" a Navy A-6 Intruder pilot asked.

"Standby for smoke," I said, turning the Bronco to the north. "Showtime, Mike."

With his familiar Marine call, Mike responded, "Oooahh."

Wheeling in on the target, I let off a smoke rocket in the center of the enemy concentration and then peeled off the target. Immediately, the Intruders rolled in and strafed the whole area and then some.

"Wolfman 45, Tonco 65 flight is one mile behind 64; we'll need smoke also," came across the radio.

"Roger," I said, lining up on the target again and firing a second rocket to the north of my first. Passing overhead, I could see a group of friendly South Vietnamese troops pinned down at a fork along a creek.

"Tonco 65 has smoke, rolling now," the responded.

Five seconds later, the area was ablaze as napalm torched the countryside, vaporizing the enemy.

"Sierra Hotel on targets," I screamed over the radio.

"Tonco 64 and 65 flight, going feet wet."

"Roger, have a good flight, and thanks for the fire."

Rolling back over the burning countryside, I surveyed the area of the strike. A mile south of the carnage, the South Vietnamese platoon was still trapped as several hundred North Vietnamese Army regulars were advancing toward their position along the banks of a creek.

"They're in trouble, aren't they?" Mike said.

"Yea, we're going to have to slow the enemy down so they can retreat. If we don't, they'll get overrun." I replied, pulling up and doing a crop duster one-eighty.

Suddenly, the enemy began launching mortars into the South Vietnamese troop positions. Well outnumbered, Mike and I knew the situation was getting desperate. We had to help them and quickly.

"Mayday! Mayday! We need help," came a cry from a South Vietnamese officer.

"Ground, Wolfman 45 is overhead," I replied, swinging my craft toward the fork in the creek.

"Steve, we won't be able to hold them off for too long," Mike said.

"I know," I responded while formulating a game plan.

"Command post, do we have any fighters in the area?" I asked.

"Negative; we're trying to get some from Danang, but it will be a while," they replied.

"Can we have the Navy hit 'em?" Mike asked.

I wondered for a second about Mike's suggestion, then said, "No, they're too close. They'll take our boys too."

"What are we going to do?" Mike responded.

"Command post, Wolfman 45, request permission to go in alone," I said.

A short pause, then Command post replied, "Wolfman 45, you're cleared in."

Zooming in low, I trained my eyes on the enemy and fired my guns near the creek's edge. The plane buffeted as our four machine guns sprayed a thousand rounds. Instantly the enemy started to disperse away from the stream.

"Good shooting," Mike said.

I pulled up and set up for another pass. Banking hard to the right, I activated two more smoke rockets and sent them into the retreating North Vietnamese.

"They're pulling back," Mike confirmed.

"Thank goodness, 'cause I'm almost out of ammo," I replied, yanking the plane around for another pass.

As I dove for the creek bank, tracers filled the night sky from all directions with several bullets impacting our fuselage. Glancing down at my gauges, everything looked normal. "I want to do one more pass to make sure they're not regrouping, "I said, "then we'll have to head home cause we're almost out of fuel."

On my fifth pass, heavy flak pounded the whole area. I knew this had to be our last pass; the anti-aircraft fire was too heavy for my light airplane.

"*Boooooom.*"

The Bronco shook violently as I tried to hold onto the controls. All the windows blew out as shrapnel showered Mike and me in the face. Turning to the left, I expected to see my engine on fire. It wasn't. It was gone entirely as twisted metal dangled from the engine mounts. The wing was on fire as flames climbed out our trailing edge.

"Hold on," I screamed as the aircraft continued shuddering from the explosion. I thought a surface-to-air missile was the only thing that could have taken my engine off.

Pulling off of the target, I checked my body, expecting to see blood flowing freely. There was none.

"Mike, are you hurt?"

"I'll live," he said, shaking. "Something hit me in the back of the head."

Struggling to save the aircraft, I lowered my seat as the wind blast ripped apart my eyelids.

"We're not going to be able to land," Mike snapped. "Take a look at the landing gear."

I glanced to the left; the gear was dangling in the airstream. I didn't care about the gear, though; my mind was on getting the fire out before we blew up.

"I got to get rid of the external tank and rockets before they catch on fire," I said, circling.

"We can't drop them on our guys," Mike fired back.

"I know; I'm heading for the water," I said, reassuring Mike.

I was racing against time now, as friendlies covered the entire area to the coast. Time slowed down as I sped for open water.

Mike got on the radio and said, "May Day! May Day! This is Wolfman 45 at Triple Nickel and 602, heading out feet wet."

The Bronco was a handful for me living up to its name. I was fighting the controls to maintain straight and level flight. The temperature on my remaining engine began to rise.

Unable to gain altitude, I kept the plane at six hundred feet until I crossed the beach and over the water. American ships and small watercraft were scattered across the black sea. At least we owned the water, I thought to myself.

Jettisoning the fuel tank and my last rockets, I prepared to eject. "Mike, are you ready to go?" I asked.

"Hold on," Mike said, glancing over his shoulder. "Crap! My parachute is shredded. The rocket blast left a hole in the cargo bay."

Damn, I thought to myself. "All right, we'll have to think of something else."

I knew I couldn't bail out and leave Mike in the aircraft to die. I glanced to the left side; the flames were subsiding. Maybe there was hope.

Quickly I turned southeast and headed down the coast. "We're going to Danang," I said. "Get on the horn and make sure they have the runway foamed for us."

"Roger," Mike responded.

From the map, the landing strips at Phu Bai and Hue were closest but had no foam capability. I didn't want to make it there and burn to death on landing.

Suddenly a loud pop came from the left wing. The fire flared again, this time a lot bigger. We were dangerously close to exploding.

"Danang's out of the question," I screamed. "I'm gonna have to ditch in the water."

"Steve, get out and save yourself," Mike yelled.

"Forget it; you'll never survive from the back seat."

I knew what Mike wanted me to do, but there was no way in hell I would let him die.

As we completed our pre-ditching checklist, I eased the aircraft into a slow descent toward the water. I fearfully remembered that no pilot from an OV-10 had ever survived a ditching before, as the plane was likely to break up as soon as it struck the water.

Setting my aimpoint one mile from a sandy beach, I pulled the power off the right engine.

The busted landing gear on the left side hit the water first, sending us cartwheeling across the waves and onto our back.

Immediately, I tried to get my safety harness undone. Upside down and holding my total weight, it became jammed. I could see Mike frantically trying to free himself out of the corner of my eye. The black darkness of the water cut the visibility down to a few feet.

Water started pouring in around my head. We we're sinking. I had to get out. I saw Mike kicking his way through a side window and making it clear as his life preservers inflated.

I felt the coolness of the water on the top of my head as I continued trying to release my safety belt. I could feel the bent handle on the release mechanism. Panicking, I raised my head to keep it out of the water. It was no use as the plane lost its will to stay afloat.

As the water completely submerged me, I took one last gulp of air and tried to crawl out of the harness. It was too tight. I could feel myself becoming dizzy as the oxygen in my lungs was running out. The latch wouldn't release.

Life was rushing by me as I felt my strength failing me. I tried to unleash myself from the monster one last time, but it wouldn't budge. I knew it was all over as bubbles trickled from my nose.

A Navy rescue helicopter immediately picked up Mike Brown.

The next day, Steve Bennett's body was recovered from the smashed cockpit of the submerged aircraft. He had no chance to escape.

Steven L. Bennett was born in Palestine, Texas, in April 1946. He entered the Air Force in 1968 and won his wings at Webb Air Force Base, Texas. In 1970, Captain Bennett completed the B-52 bomber training course at Castle Air Force Base, California.

He graduated from the FAC and fighter training course at Cannon Air Force Base, New Mexico, before reporting to Vietnam in 1972. The 26-year-old pilot had been in combat less than three months before his Medal of Honor mission. The Medal was awarded posthumously. Captain Bennett also won the Air Medal with three oak leaf clusters.

CHAPTER 8

Captains Bob Pardo and Earl Aman
F-4 Phantom

This story is well-known in the Air Force community. It is a remarkable display of courage and airmanship to help out a fellow buddy in his time of need.

* * *

March 10, 1967, brought clear skies as I checked in my wingman, Captain Earl Aman, over the radio. Aman's back-seater, 1st Lieutenant Robert Houghton, gave me a visual thumbs up that everything was okay. We both were assigned to the 433rd Tactical Fighter Squadron at Ubon Royal Thai Air Force Base in Thailand. We'd flown mission after mission together in our F-4 Phantoms but had yet to go against the enemy.

I knew today would be different. Our elusive target was the only steel production complex in North Vietnam at Thai Nguyen. Low clouds protected the complex during the nine days Aman and I tried to reduce it to rubble just north of Hanoi. Intelligence sources reported a half-dozen surface-to-air missile sites and more than 1,000 anti-aircraft guns surrounding the area.

"Steve, you feeling lucky today," I asked.

"Yes, sir," First Lieutenant Steve Wayne, my back-seater, replied. "Let's go hunting."

"Did the strike force get airborne?" I inquired.

"Affirmative; they took off five minutes ago," he responded.

Today, Aman and I were joined by other F-105s and F-4s to take out the site targeted by the Joint Chiefs of Staff. My job was to protect the other aircraft in the strike force from MiGs. Our F-4s were loaded with missiles and bombs. If we encountered any threatening North

Vietnamese MiGs, we would use our missiles; if not, we would drop everything we had on the steel mill.

Approaching the target, Steve announced, "Screens clear."

"That's a little odd, don't you think?" I replied.

"Yea, you'd figure they'd have a few MiGs patrolling the skies today," he replied.

"Well, keep your eyes open," I said. "Do you have the coordinates to the target?"

Steve fired back, "Come right, fifteen degrees."

"Aman, come right fifteen degrees," I said over the radio. "We'll hit the target on my mark."

"Roger," he replied.

"Thirty seconds to target," Steve's voice said in a higher tone. "Anti-aircraft fire on your right side."

"I see 'em," I replied as the stream of bullets wavered across the sky, trying to meet my flight path.

It was a picture-perfect day, and I could see clearly across the valley. Suddenly, ordinance from the main strike force started pounding into the hillside.

"Ten seconds," Steve said, now yelling over the intercom.

I didn't respond as another stream of anti-aircraft fire raced across the sky from my left. Pulling my aircraft up ninety degrees, I skirted the shells. On my right wing, Aman didn't have enough time to react.

"I'm hit! I'm hit!" Captain Aman screamed.

Slamming the controls to the right, I brought my aircraft upright to see liquid spraying from Aman's aircraft. Glancing back, I could see our target.

"Time?" I asked.

"Five seconds," Steve responded.

Aman was in serious trouble as we approached our target, but he stuck to my wing like glue. "Two, how are you doing?" I inquired.

"I'm okay! I'm okay! Let's hit the target and get the hell out of here," he said.

I knew he wasn't okay. He could jettison his bombs and head home, but that wasn't the Aman I knew.

I took a deep breath and said, "All right, drop on my mark.

Three. . . . Two . . . One" as bombs from both our aircraft headed straight for the main factory. Suddenly, I could see tracers zipping across our flight path as several *thunks* pelted my fuselage.

"Were hit!" Steve yelled over the intercom.

I gripped the controls tightly as we pulled away from the steel mill. Several warning lights flashed brightly in my cockpit. I moved my controls around, and everything responded normally. Captain Aman wasn't as lucky. The barrage of anti-aircraft fire found his precious fuel tanks, draining 5,000 pounds in less than a minute.

"We're hit hard," Houghton said over the radio.

I set a course for us straight for the air refueling aircraft. My mind raced, calculating the distance to the Laotian border. There was no way Aman was going to make it, I thought. It was a sure bet he'd have to bail out over hostile territory.

"Lead, we're not going to make it," Aman said, as if reading my mind.

"Just keep going; I'll figure something out," I responded. I was running out of options faster than Aman was running out of fuel. I had to try something, anything.

Suddenly, an option came to me. "Two, take the lead," I directed.

"Roger, I got the lead," Aman replied, moving in front of me.

"Lead, I'm going to try and put my nose in your drag chute compartment," I said.

A long silence from Aman, "Roger."

Sliding my F-4 underneath Aman's, I tried to get close enough to his drag chute compartment, but too much jet wash was coming off his plane. There was no way it was going to work. I had to think of something else.

Another thought came to me. "Aman, drop your tailhook!" I shouted desperately.

"What?" Aman replied.

"Your tailhook. Drop it! I'm going to try to push you along," I ordered.

He did not reply this time.

What I suggested had never been done before, and the Phantom wasn't designed for such a maneuver. Aman's tailhook lowered and locked into place, controlled by hydraulics. It swayed a little in the slipstream of the F-4's twin J-75 engines.

I pulled in behind and below, slowly creeping forward, hoping to lodge his tailhook against the leading edge of my windshield. I knew the windshield glass was strong enough to withstand mild contact, but only mild. I knew my windshield was over an inch thick, but one solid jolt might plant Aman's tail hook in my lap.

His tailhook kissed the front of my windshield while flying at two hundred and fifty knots. My heart was pounding as it grazed back and forth, scraping across the glass. For a moment, I would get it stabilized, and then it would fall off. It just wouldn't work. There was just too much jet wash with Aman's engines running.

"Two, we only got a minute of fuel left," Aman relayed.

"Copy," I replied. Thinking as fast as I could, I responded, "Lead, shut down both of your engines."

Aman immediately shut down both J-75s as I inched forward and made contact. It worked. With no jet wash, I could stabilize his tailhook on my windshield and push him along. We were now flying as one aircraft on both my engines.

Slowly, I pushed both of my throttles forward. I kept the tailhook lodged on my windshield, tripling our glide range. Our sink rate had decreased to only 1,000 feet per minute now. We might make it, I thought.

Without warning, the tailhook slipped off. Fighting the wind and the sink rate, I repositioned my aircraft underneath the his tailhook. All of a sudden, I heard my Master Caution horn go off.

"Fire in our left engine," hollered Steve.

"Crap!" Everything was starting to go downhill. The damage I sustained earlier began showing signs. My fire warning light indicated a probable external fire near the left engine.

"Steve, I'm gonna shut down the number two engine to extinguish the fire and then try a restart."

"Roger, I'll guard the right engine," he replied.

Reaching over, I pulled the left throttle back over the detent as the RPMs wound down. The engine cranked back up after pressing the start button. The fire warning light was off, but the internal temperature increased to over 1,000 degrees Celsius. It should've read only 600. I quickly surmised that it could only mean one of two things: the flame holders or the burner cans inside the engine had ruptured. We had an uncontrolled fire that could explode inside the engine and possibly destroy our airplane.

"It's too hot; I'm going to shut it down again," I stated.

A minute later, I glanced down only to see that our sink rate had increased to 2,000 feet per minute. We weren't going to make it on my one engine. I had no choice but to try and get that left engine back started.

I said, "Restarting the left engine."

I hit the left engine start switch again. It restarted, and I resumed pushing Aman, hoping everything would be okay. Less than a minute later, however, the fire warning light returned. It was no use. I had to shut the engine down again; otherwise, I might kill us all. I gently pulled the throttle back over the detent—this time for good.

We flew another ten minutes on my right engine. The whole time, Steve was on the radio calling for an air refueling tanker, hoping Aman could link up and get a pull from the large aerial gas station. But time was running out, and the tanker wouldn't make it in time.

"Approaching Black River," said Steve.

I could see the winding river passing underneath our nose. A sigh of relief passed over me; finally, we had reached Laos.

"We can't make it back to the base, Bob," Steve said, "we're too low and descending."

"I know," glancing at my altimeter. We were only 6,000 feet above the ground, and I couldn't sustain pushing Aman much longer. My F-4 was running low on fuel, and with 6,000 feet of altitude, we only had two minutes of flying time left.

"This is Tanker support; several A-1 Skyraiders are proceeding in your direction; say intentions?" came over the radio.

"Tanker support, my lead aircraft can't make Ubon," I replied. "He's gonna have to bail out south of the Black River."

"Tanker support copies, we'll direct your rescue."

"Aman, that's all I can give you," I said reluctantly over the radio. "You're going to have to bailout."

"Thanks, Bob, you're cleared off," he replied gratefully.

I pulled back and off to the right of Aman and Houghton's aircraft. Within a second, their canopies blew off as two ejection seats went up the rails. As their parachute opened, I hit the throttle on my remaining engine and headed for a US Special Forces camp I knew was ahead.

Two minutes later, our fuel was gone, and both our engines flamed out. Flying like a giant rock in the sky, we heading for the ground and fast. I couldn't wait any longer as I yelled, "Bailout! Bailout!"

Steve ejected immediately. A second later, I reached down and pulled the black and yellow striped handles. The G-forces from the ejection were incredible. I strained to keep my eyes open, but the force was too great.

Floating down in my chute, I saw our F-4 slam into the side of a mountain, creating a tremendous explosion. Suddenly, below me, villagers started shooting.

Hitting the ground, I found Steve as the rescue helicopters were coming over the mountain. Within a few minutes, both of us were inside the comfort of the rescue chopper heading back to Ubon.

Later, I found out Aman had landed on the back side of a cliff. Houghton, who'd suffered a vertebra compression fracture during his ejection, was floating directly toward a Laotian village. The villagers yelled and pointed at Houghton as he dropped into a tree. His chute snagged on a limb and stopped barely inches from the ground. Then the villagers started shooting at him. Unstrapping his harness and scared to death, he ran as fast as could

While Houghton was running from the villagers, Aman had his own problems. Wearing slick-soled boots, he tried to scramble up a hill to escape the villagers but couldn't. Every step forward he took, he slid back two.

Finally, the unmistakable roar of Skyraiders swooped low over the mountains on top of them with rescue choppers close behind. When the villagers headed for cover, the helicopters hoisted them both inside. Four hours later, they joined us at Ubon.

Some people felt I should have let Earl and Bob eject and take their chances so that I could land my aircraft safely. I thought that was a bunch of crap. He was my wingman.

CHAPTER 9

Lt. Colonel William A. Jones III

A-1 Skyraider

Medal of Honor

In the FAC role, the A-1 pilot was an aerial observer and controller. In constant radio contact with Army units in his sector, he warned of enemy ambushes and controlled fast-moving fighters on strikes.

The airman downed deep in enemy territory, and the embattled foot soldier caught in a Vietcong (VC) crossfire often depended on the Skyraider for their lives.

Bill Jones has to be a hero in everyone's book. Another veteran of World War II, he displays his experience on the battlefield of Vietnam. This story of bravery is genuinely remarkable. I think you will agree.

* * *

With helmet and gloves in hand, I slammed my office door shut as the glass window shuttered. The sign on the door read, "602nd Special Operations Squadron Commander."

Turning to my executive officer, "I'm going flying," I said. "If anything comes up, put it in my inbox."

"See ya later, Commander, have a safe flight," he replied.

"Thanks," I responded.

Life as a squadron commander was murder. I was not too fond of all the paperwork that went along with the job while all my young pilots were out gallivanting across the skies. Vietnam would be my last war, I thought to myself, walking out to my A-1. Twenty-three years and three wars were enough.

An assortment of thirty A-1s lined the ramp as I threw my flight gear down at the foot of the crew ladder.

"Joe, is she ready to go?" I asked.

Startled, Joe hit his head on the bottom of the fuselage as he came out from underneath the plane.

"Yes sir, she's in tip-top shape," he replied, wiping his oily hands on his pant legs.

Strapping in, I called, "Sandy 01 check."

"Two . . . Three . . . Four," the rest of the formation responded.

As dawn broke over Nakhon Phanom Royal Thai Air Force Base, we lifted off, leaving the jungles of Thailand behind. It was my ninety-eighth combat mission.

"Sandy 01 flight, tighten up the formation," I called to the other three aircraft.

Proceeding westbound, I settled into my seat and reviewed the pickup area we were assigned today.

Two hours earlier, I had gotten a call that an F-4 pilot had bailed out near Dong Hoi, and they needed us to run a search and rescue operation to extract him. My Sandy flight was supposed to provide air support for a helicopter pickup.

Passing the border into North Vietnam, I called, "Sandy 01 flight, in country."

Each of my wingmen responded by rocking their wings.

Ten minutes later, we arrived northwest of Dong Hoi. "Sandy 03 and 04, go high into orbit," I ordered.

"Three . . . Four," as the two ships peeled off and zoomed skyward.

Sending three and four high would keep them out of range of the enemy's anti-aircraft weapons and conserve fuel. As their squadron commander, I was responsible for being the first in the "Hot Zone."

"Sandy 02, let's go down for a look," I ordered.

"Roger," Captain Paul Meeks responded.

Dumping my nose, I headed into the valley and started combing the last known area of the downed pilot.

"Sandy 01 flight, this is Liner 22," an airborne F-4 pilot said.

"Liner 22, go ahead?" I replied.

"We've established radio contact with Charter 02 Alpha on the ground," he said. "Follow us inbound, and we'll rock our wings at his location."

"Wilco," I replied, spotting the fast-moving Phantom two miles in front of us. Shoving the throttle to the wall, I used cutoff angles to close the distance on the faster F-4.

Established two hundred yards behind him, we followed Liner 22 back down through the valley. Two miles later, Liner 22 aggressively rocked his wings back and forth as I noted the position.

"Sandy 01 has position," I called out.

Reversing my course back down the valley again, I expected the enemy gunners to open fire. They didn't. The area seemed too peaceful, and I started to get that uneasy feeling.

"Charter 02 Alpha, this is Sandy 01," I said over the radio, "do you copy?"

No response.

I repeated the call, but still Charter 02 Alpha didn't reply. This was odd, I thought to myself, had his radio gone dead, and he couldn't talk anymore? Maybe the enemy was so close to him that he couldn't afford to make a transmission?

Paul and I circled the area for the next hour, trying to contact the pilot, but to no avail.

"Sandy 01, this is Roper 44," an F-100 pilot radioed.

"Sandy 01, go," I responded.

"I have contact with Charter 02 Alpha; he's eight east of your position," the pilot stated.

Crap, I thought to myself; Liner 22 had the wrong location. We had wasted almost an hour.

"Sandy 01 and 02 proceeding eastbound," I called out over the readio.

I gave Paul the visual hand signal for a right echelon as we ducked around the mountains tracking eastbound.

The F-100 pilot continued, "Sandy 01, the enemy has a 37-millimeter gun at the top of the hill above Charter 02 Alpha position."

"Sandy copies," I replied. I told myself that that would explain why it was so quite in the wrong valley.

I spotted the F-100 circling high overhead a few miles later. "Charter 02 Alpha, do you see me overhead?" I inquired.

"Negative; there are no aircraft above me," he responded.

Here we go again, I thought.

"Lead, Route 137's off to the left," Paul blurted out.

"I see it," I replied, "let's stay on this side. I'm sure they have it heavily defended."

Swinging back down the valley again, I began widening my search pattern. The weather started to deteriorate as a cloud deck now covered the tops of the mountains. The terrain became more challenging to fly in as the rugged hills rose sharply from the valley floor.

Instantly, small arms fire erupted from every direction. Then "*Kaboom*" as an explosion burst from underneath my fuselage.

The North Vietnamese had my range nailed. Smoke filled the cockpit as I regained control of the aircraft and jinked from side to side to spoil their gunner's aim.

As the smoke cleared, I scanned the engine instruments and visually checked the aircraft. I was surprised to see all the flight controls and the engine performing normal.

"Sandy 01, you're trailing smoke," Paul cried out.

Again I checked my instruments. "01 normal from the cockpit," I replied, easing Paul's fears.

Time was against me now. I needed to locate the survivor before the North Vietnamese could beef up their defenses.

"More guns at two o'clock, halfway up the hill," Paul screamed.

"I got 'em," I called, spotting the emplacement. Swinging away from the guns, I headed back to the south. More ground fire erupted as Paul split off my wing.

Spinning around, I started another pass down the valley.

Suddenly, Charter 02 Alpha screamed, "I have an A-1 directly overhead."

"Bingo!" I yelled over the mic as I banked up my plane and saw him directly below me. I finally found my man.

"Charter 02 Alpha's position is—"

"Ping . . . ping . . . ping," as bullets ripped holes into the top of my engine. Again the enemy gunners were homing in on my position, but this time the barrage came from the top of a small hill from my right. The gun emplacement was only a few hundred yards from the downed pilot.

"Guns, high right," I hollered.

Immediately, I tried swinging my nose toward the source, but I was going too fast to unleash any weapons upon them. I couldn't risk calling in the fighters because the enemy's gun position was too close to Charter 02 Alpha.

"Sandy 02, let's take them out ourselves," I yelled, pulling a tight five-G turn and reversing course.

"02 copies," Paul said. "I'm at the north end; I'll be there in a minute."

Diving toward my tormentors, I triggered off two rockets and held the cannon button down, spraying the area with shells. Passing overhead, I yanked back on the stick and set up for another pass.

On my second run, a 14.5-millimeter riddled my underbelly.

Intense heat spilled out from behind my seat. Behind me, flames had ignited my ejection seat rocket motor, sending a plume of orange fire out the back end of my airplane.

"Sandy 02, I'm in trouble," I hollered.

The instrument panel became clouded with smoke again as flames engulfed my entire cockpit. I pulled up for altitude and headed out of the gauntlet.

Instantly, Paul was on my left wing, "-01, Bailout! Bailout!" he directed. "You're gonna blow."

Without waiting any longer, I reached down and grabbed the ejection handle with my right hand, and pulled. I heard a large explosion as the canopy flew off my plane, but nothing else happened.

An eternity passed as I expected the ejection seat to follow the canopy. It didn't. The ejection seat rocket had malfunctioned. I thought this couldn't be happening to me.

The fire burned wildly as the blast of fresh air from the missing canopy hit the cockpit. I reached down and grabbed the secondary escape handle. It didn't work either.

"Sandy 02, my ejection system is inop," I screamed.

"01, jump over the side," came the reply from my wingman.

My oxygen mask started to burn through as searing flames pounced around my face. My hands were painfully scorched and looked like mozzarella cheese.

"Sandy 01, Bailout!" another pilot cried out.

Then, miraculously, the flames died in the blackened cockpit. I couldn't bailout, I thought to myself. It would just complicate the rescue mission if I did.

My mind raced on what to do. I was the only one who knew the location of the Charter 02 Alpha. I had to let someone know. Keying up the mic, I said, "Char—"

"Sandy 01, get out!" came over the airways.

"Damn it," I yelled as someone cut me off. "Charter 02 Alpha is . . ." Static, as my transmitter went dead. I looked down at the radio; it was as black as burnt toast.

With one hand, I tried to find my emergency radio in my survival vest as I flew with the other. No luck; it had melted into the green mesh of my vest. All my options were fading away.

With one thought in mind, I turned my plane west and flew toward Nakhon Phanom. I would have to wait until I landed there to report the exact location of Carter 02 Alpha.

Sandy 02 took the lead as I tapped my head and pointed forward. Immediately, he sped up and headed home as I stuck to him like glue.

Excruciating pain from the burns I sustained began trickling through my body. I ground my teeth together, trying to take my mind off the pain as Nakhon Phanom lay forty agonizing minutes away.

The initial explosion had shattered two-thirds of my windscreen. My face swelled up as the windblast pummeled me at a hundred and fifty miles an hour. I could feel my eyes slowly swelling shut.

As we approached Nakhon Phanom, the weather began to deteriorate. Sliding in closer to Sandy 02, I stayed right on his wing as he set up for an instrument approach to the runway.

Halfway through the clouds, I threw my landing gear down. I wasn't surprised when I didn't get two green indications. Feverishly, I started cranking the emergency system down. Tears flooded my partially opened eyes as I tried to stay on Paul's wing.

Finally, we broke out of the weather, and Paul did a "go-around" to let me land first. Fire trucks line the infield as I set up for the landing. Struggling with the controls, I eased the plane onto the pavement and stopped at the end of the runway.

Immediately, Colonel Leonard Volet, the Base Commander, ran up to the cockpit.

"Bill, I can't believe you didn't jump over the side," he said, screaming at me. "God! Look at you; you're burnt to a crisp."

"Get me a map," I yelled; "I'll show you where Charter 02 is."

"Don't worry about that; we've got to get you to the hospital."

"No! I'm not going until you get me a map," I replied sternly.

"Okay. Okay. We'll get a map, but at least get out of the cockpit," the Colonel replied.

With Colonel Volet's help, I struggled to get my arms out of the parachute straps. "Ahhhh," I hollered, as the pain was almost unbearable.

Haphazardly I made it down the ladder as Colonel Volet produced a map. I circled the downed pilot's position and all the enemy gun emplacements.

"You're a crazy and stupid fool," Volet said, "You know that, don't you?"

"I know," I replied. It was too painful to smile.

Near Dong Hoi, the massive rescue effort continued. Later that day, Carter 02 Alpha was picked up.

Born in 1922, William A. Jones III graduated from the University of Virginia in 1942. He attended the US Military Academy at West Point, graduating in 1945.

Colonel Jones won his wings in 1945 and flew with the Strategic Air Command and a Troop Carrier Wing, with overseas duty in the Philippine Islands and Europe.

Before the Medal of Honor mission in 1968, Colonel Jones flew 98 combat missions from Thailand. In November 1969, William A. Jones III was killed in a private airplane crash near Woodbridge, Virginia.

CHAPTER 10

Captain Hilliard A. Wilbanks

O-1E Bird Dog

Medal of Honor

A forward air controller continually flies over the sector of operations of an Army unit. He soon becomes intimately familiar with the terrain, villages, roads, and streams, and his trained eye can detect unusual or suspicious movements. Most forward air controllers have also flown fighters. Familiarity with fighter tactics pays off when they request close air support and control fighter airstrikes.

The forward air controller was respected and feared by the Vietcong. The enemy knew that whatever area he circled, the jungle could erupt from the devastating firepower at his command.

The elusive enemy, the absence of fixed battle lines, and the rugged terrain and weather in Vietnam made effective air and ground coordination mandatory. The forward air controller provided both protection and offensive firepower for friendly ground troops. We were usually outnumbered when the enemy chose to make contact. At airfields in Vietnam, fighter and attack pilots were on round-the-clock alert, ready to scramble whenever the Army required immediate close air support.

Because of the unique nature of the Vietnam War and the evolution of flexible and responsive air support, it was the first conflict in Air Force history in which a forward air controller earned the Medal of Honor.

From a quote by President Johnson during Captain Wilbanks's posthumous Medal of Honor dedication, "Flying through a hail of withering fire at treetop level, Captain Wilbanks passed directly over the advancing enemy and inflicted many casualties by firing his rifle out of the side window of his aircraft." This statement only shows how some heroes will do whatever it takes to accomplish their mission.

* * *

"Wilbanks." my burly old Operations Officer yelled across the briefing room.

I cupped my hands over my forehead. Why did he always have to pick me? I only had two months remaining in the country until I would be with my wife and kids in the States.

"You're up again, Hilliard," another pilot beside me said, chuckling.

Finally, glancing up in my best military voice, I said, "Yes, sir!"

"I want you up tonight over Bao Lac and Di Linh," my Ops officer said.

"What's the problem?" I asked, standing up and walking over to him.

"Last night, the Vietcong ambushed the 23rd South Vietnamese Ranger Battalion and a small detachment of American advisers," he explained. "Earlier today, they decimated one platoon of South Vietnamese troops while hitting two other companies from a hillside. If the damn weather had cooperated, we'd been able to help the Rangers. A lot of Americans and South Vietnamese were killed in the firefight."

I could feel the lump in my throat rising as the sobering announcement silenced the room. We were losing hundreds of men a day in the jungles. It was tough on my squadron when we could have prevented it.

The Ops officer continued, "Anyway, they set a trap using the local tea plantation workers to help them dig foxholes and bunkers to the west of Di Linh," pointing to the map on the wall. "I want you to get out there and patrol that area because I think they may try the same thing tonight."

Okay, I'll take off in an hour," I said, turning around and heading out the door.

I often flew over the central highlands near Bao Lac and Di Linh. These two small cities were located a hundred miles northeast of Saigon and were surrounded by rolling hills, forests, and an occasional plantation. The tribal Montagnards, or "mountain people" as we called them, were the chief inhabitants of this region.

While doing the preflight on my "Bird Dog," my thoughts again traveled to my wife and kids. Ten months had been my longest time away from them, except for my stint in Korea. I couldn't wait till April when I would be on that Freedom Bird for the last time. I was getting tired of facing the eyes of death every day.

Easing myself into the seat, I hit the start button as the propeller wound up. Taxing out onto the dirt airstrip, I did my best to avoid all the small potholes from the recent rains. The propeller splashed up dirty water on the side of my plane, adding to the brown camouflage. Soon, I forgot about seeing my family as my mind focused on my mission.

Just as the sun set, I was on my 488th combat mission. Skimming across the trees at a hundred feet, I kept my Cessna moving, banking back and forth in case someone wanted to take a potshot at me. Approaching Di Linh, I saw two helicopter gunships and another Bird Dog hovering west of the village.

"Gunships, this is Bird Dog Two on station," I called out.

"Roger Bird Dog Two, contact the Rangers," the other Bird Dog replied.

Circling overhead, I spotted the Rangers slowly advancing through the flat area of the tea plantation. Scanning the area before them, I switch to a different frequency.

"Twenty-third Rangers, this is Bird Dog Two with you," I said.

"I got ya," Captain R. J. Wooten replied. "How's our front side look?"

"I don't see anything yet," I replied, still searching the terrain. The plantation offered no protection or cover.

I took the area to the west near the hills while the other Bird Dog positioned himself east of me. Flying across the valley, I could see the lead element of the Rangers leaving the plantation and heading up the slope of the low-lying hills.

Suddenly, I saw some movement in the brush halfway up the hill. Banking the Cessna around hard to the left, I wanted another look. Straining my eyes, I saw movement everywhere. My God, there were thousands of Vietcong dug into the side of the hill. Well hidden in camouflage foxholes, they were patiently waiting for the advancing Rangers.

"They're setting a tr—" I screamed but was cut off.

Instantly, ground fire erupted from all around, cutting off my transmission. Muzzle flashes lit up the sky.

Realizing I had found them, the enemy decided to spring the trap instead of waiting. I could hear the low rhythmic thumps on the bottom of my aircraft as machine-gun rounds found their mark.

The lead Ranger elements dropped to the ground as they were pinned down at the base of the hills. Mortar shells began impacting near the main unit in the center of the plantation, sending them flat on their faces in the wide-open field.

I yanked my Cessna in and out of the trees so they couldn't get an easy shot off. After spotting what I thought was their main concentration of troops, I fired a white phosphorus rocket. The smoke rose from the hillside.

"Gunships hit the smoke! Hit the smoke!" I screamed.

"I see the target," one of the gunships replied.

I could see the two helicopter gunships wheeling in toward the enemy, spraying the entire area, but there were just too many Vietcong troops in the hills. After a barrage of shells and rockets, both gunships pulled away.

"We're hit! We're hit!" a third chopper to the east responded. "They got our hydraulics."

The .50-caliber enemy guns had homed in on them. I could see smoke trailing the chopper as it limped away to the east. It would be an easy target without an escort.

"Gunship One and Two, escort him out of here," I yelled over the radio.

"Roger," they replied.

"Bird Dog Two, this is Bird Dog One, two flights of friendly fighters are on their way."

Thank God, I thought. We desperately needed more firepower, or the Rangers would not make it.

Suddenly, I saw more movement out of the corner of my eye. Glancing through the smoke, I saw the Vietcong abandoning their foxholes. With only bayonets and their knives, they began to charge down the slopes toward the badly outnumbered Rangers.

I had to do something fast. The Rangers had no idea how many Vietcong were heading in their direction. Hurling my plane back down on the deck toward the enemy, I lined up for another pass.

"Bird Dog, it's too hot. Get out of there," Captain Wooten hollered over the radio.

But I knew I couldn't leave. I had to draw the enemy's attention away from the Rangers. There would be scant hope for them until the fighters arrived.

Closing in on my target, I popped another smoke rocket into their midst. Flying directly over the confused Vietcong, they started firing at me instead of the Rangers. It wasn't exactly what I wanted them to do. A couple more *"thunks"* ripped through my plane as I flew over the backside of the hills.

Reversing direction, I had their full attention as I fired another smoke rocket into their main force. I had become the hunter now, but only for a short time, with only one rocket left. Hopefully, it would be enough time for the fighters to arrive.

I fired my last rocket less than a hundred feet above the trees. Even the Vietcong knew I was out of rockets as they stood in the open firing at me.

"Bird Dog One, how much longer for the fighters?" I inquired.

"They'll be here in ten minutes," he responded.

Ten minutes, I mumbled to myself. That's too long. The Vietcong would be upon the Rangers within ten minutes, preventing the fighters from doing any good.

I had to come up with something else. Glancing over in the right seat, I saw the automatic rifle I carried as a survival weapon with a full clip. It was my only option. I had never tried to fly the plane and fire my rifle out the window, but there had to be a first time for everything.

Scanning the area again, I saw the Vietcong starting down the hill, knowing I was helpless. Pointing my plane straight at them, I let go of the controls and hoisted my rifle out the window.

With one hand on the trigger and the other opening the window, I began firing at them. Immediately, the Vietcong ducked back down into their foxholes. Off-balanced and confused, they began firing at me again. I became an easier target for them since I couldn't maneuver the airplane and fire my rifle simultaneously.

Just as the plane was about to hit the treetops, I emptied the clip and grabbed the controls to recover the aircraft. I pulled up just in time to avoid a collision with a tall pine. I rolled hard right and reloaded another clip into my rifle.

"Bird Dog Two, you're too close. Get out of there!" Bird Dog One yelled.

I didn't respond as I threw the window open again and started firing. More bullets hit the side of my aircraft. My luck wouldn't hold out long before a stray bullet found my fuel tanks.

"Where in the hell were those fighters?" I screamed to myself.

Reaching over for my last clip, I slammed it into the rifle and made one more pass. After this, I wouldn't be able to help the Rangers anymore. Only the fighters would be able to save them now.

Rolling out, I only got four shots off before I felt a stinging pain in my chest. Instinctively, I dropped the rifle and tried holding onto the plane. I could feel my world swallowing me up. My vision started to blur as I tried to control the aircraft.

The plane bolted up, banked to the right, and started a slow descending turn. All my strength was gone as I slumped forward on the controls. I couldn't fly the plane as it was on its own now.

I saw the lead Ranger element pass beneath my plane as I crashed into no man's land between the two Armies.

Slumped over and barely conscious, a couple of minutes later, I heard an American voice saying, "Hold on, buddy, I'm going to get you out of here."

I could hardly keep my eyes open as blood drenched my entire body.

"I need a rescue chopper right now!" the voice screamed into the radio.

Grabbing me by my flight suit, an Army Captain dragged me away from the burning wreckage of my aircraft. Two other Rangers showed up and tugged on my clothes as they moved me down the hill toward the other Rangers.

While being dragged on my back, I saw multiple rockets fired from two gunships. I wondered if they were the two I sent away to escort the damaged chopper.

Dozing in and out of consciousness, I watched the gunships hover overhead, trying to land. Four times they were unsuccessful. Each time the Vietcong guns drove them off.

Suddenly, the entire area exploded as two F-4 Phantoms arrived and raked the Vietcong with a 20-millimeter cannon fire. Finally, they had arrived.

The next thing I remember was inside the helicopter.

"Hold on," a man said. "We're taking you to the treatment center in Bao Lac. We'll be there in a few minutes. Just hold on."

I felt at peace with myself. The pain had subsided, but I couldn't keep my eyes open anymore as I thought about my wife and kids. I would never get to see them again.

In 1950, Hilliard Wilbanks graduated from high school in Cornelia, Georgia. He immediately enlisted in the Air Force and served as a security guard during the Korean War. He began flying in 1954 as an aviation cadet at Laredo, Texas, winning the gold bars of a second lieutenant and the silver wings of an Air Force pilot. Lieutenant Wilbanks flew first as an instructor pilot and then as a fighter pilot in the F-86 Sabre Jet that had become famous in air combat over Korea.

He also served as an aircraft maintenance officer in Alaska and Las Vegas, Nevada.

After training at Hurlburt Field near Fort Walton Beach, Florida, the fighter pilot became a FAC. After his assignment to Vietnam in April 1966, the 33-year-old earned the Distinguished Flying Cross and the Air Medal with 18 oak leaf clusters. Hilliard was awarded the Medal of Honor posthumously.

SURVIVAL

"The will to live."

In the back of every pilot's mind is the possibility of leaving their aircraft. One minute they are nice and cozy in the cockpit, and then they are hit with freezing temperatures. Military pilots often don't get to choose the type of environment they will fly in. From freezing Arctic temperatures to the unbearable heat of the Amazon jungle, US pilots have traversed all areas of the world to defend American objectives.

No matter how much preparation goes into planning a mission over hostile terrain, the unthinkable can and does happen. A crewmember can never be adequately prepared to handle the unforgiving climate of Mother Nature. The following two stories show how a crewmember's will to survive can overcome even the most extreme conditions.

Survival stories have been told thousands of times during a military pilot's annual egress training. Stories where the individual gave up and committed suicide just hours before rescue aircraft was on the scene. These two men would never give up.

It is said that the only thing worse than ejecting in the frozen Arctic is ejecting alone in the frozen Arctic.

CHAPTER 11

1st Lieutenant Leon Crane
B-24 Liberator

I couldn't wait for the movie when I first read this story. In the first of two survival stories, Leon Crane shows us what it takes to give one hundred percent. Here is a remarkable hero with an unrelenting desire and will to live. There are very few stories like this one in existence.

* * *

We began assembling early in the morning, before daybreak. Our specially instrumented B-24D was standing ready on the Ladd Field in Fairbanks, Alaska, as the snow started to fall. I loved the four-engine airplane everyone called the Liberator. It was the only airplane I ever wanted to fly, and I couldn't wait to move into the aircraft commander's seat from my co-pilot position. As I finished my walk around, I saw the rest of the crew for '910' walking out onto the cold ramp.

"Leon, how's everything with the airplane?" Second Lieutenant Harold E. 'Hos' Hoskins asked.

I looked at my aircraft commander, who was a little older than me. "Fine, I checked everything, and nothing appears out of the ordinary," I said.

"Great! Let's go get these tests done," he responded cheerfully.

I threw the dirty rag down that I used to check the oil and jumped into the co-pilot seat. These "test missions" were always a little nerve-racking to fly. After maintenance completed their recent overhaul, we had to take the ole Liberators up and ensure everything worked before sending the planes off to the war in the Pacific. I watched my flight engineer, Master Sergeant Richard Pompeo, and radio operator Sergeant Ralph Wenz climb aboard. Technical engineer

First Lieutenant James B. Seibert was the last man up the ladder who would monitor the flight tests for us.

At 0940, Hos Hoskins pulled back on the yoke as aircraft "910" climbed into the cold, arctic air. It was four days before Christmas, and I started thinking of the last-minute Christmas shopping I still had to do. I settled in my seat as we were all strapped in and on oxygen. We headed east at 10,000 feet.

"Starting my first series of tests," Lieutenant Seibert said over the intercom.

At 1003 AWT, Sergeant Wenz came on the radio and made our first position report. "Big Delta, Aircraft 910, forty miles southeast of Ladd Field, checking in."

"Roger Aircraft 910, this is Big Delta. We have your position plotted; stay in contact," they replied.

"Roger, 910 out," Wenz responded.

At 15,000 feet, we punched through a thin layer of clouds as Hos flew the plane. I couldn't wait to get my hands on the controls.

Ten minutes later, Hos said, "Leveling off at 20,000 feet," as he pushed the yoke over.

"Lt. Seibert, how're your tests running?" I asked.

"Getting ready to run the second series now," he replied.

I watched Hos keep the plane straight and level until Seibert finished with the second test. The weather was building toward the south, and a second cloud deck was above us.

Five minutes later, Seibert returned and said, "I've finished my second set of tests back here; you're cleared to maneuver."

Hos leaned forward in the seat and looked upward as he asked, "Leon, help me find a hole to punch through?"

I systematically searched the sky, but there was not a hole anywhere to be found, only clouds in every direction. Hos flew around in a circle waiting for a hole to appear.

"Big Delta, Aircraft 910 reporting in," Sergeant Wenz said.

"Aircraft 910, go ahead," Big Delta replied.

"Aircraft 910 is flying a random flight path and clear of the clouds southeast of Big Delta. Time is 1100 AWT," Wenz continued.

"Leon, why don't you fly for a little while?" Hos directed.

"Sure," I replied as I anxiously grabbed the yoke. I felt the power beneath me as all four engines were purring. So far, everything was working like clockwork, except for the weather.

A little before noon, Hos spotted a hole big enough to climb through and took the plane back from me. He pushed the throttles to maximum power and started a climbing turn to get through the hole.

"Let's try to level off above these clouds so Lt. Seibert can complete his last series of tests," Hos remarked.

It was during this circling climb that things started going wrong and fast. I turned to Hos and said, "I don't think we can make it through that hole. It's closing up pretty fast."

"We can make it," he replied confidently.

At 23,000 feet, the hole closed up, and we entered the clouds. Now we were completely IFR and in the weather without visual references. All of a sudden, I could hear the engine noise level drop.

"Number one engine has failed," yelled flight engineer Pompeo.

Hos pushed the nose over with the loss of thrust to level the aircraft, but we were still in a left-hand turn.

Somebody in the back screamed, "We have a vacuum selector valve frozen in the number one position."

Both our eyes immediately went to the center panel. "Crap! Co, check the gauges," Hos commanded abruptly.

I quickly scanned all the engine instruments. "All of our gauges are frozen because of the vacuum pump failure," I replied.

The backup airspeed and altimeter were the only ones working.

Hos started recycling switches and banging his hand on the gauges. I watched in vain as Hos tried to get them to read correctly. Then I looked at the altimeter. It was spinning out of control.

In the seat of my pants, I could feel the airplane turning. "Hos, we're in a spin to the left!" I screamed.

Hos replied, "Leon, get on the controls and help me."

I came on the controls, but noticed they were very sluggish. It took all our strength for Hos and me to try and overcome the spin.

Over the intercom, I could hear Wenz, "Big Delta, Aircraft 910 has lost our number one engine, and we are in a spin. I repeat, we lost our number one en—"

At 20,000 feet, we broke out of the clouds. Hos and I manhandled the controls enough to recover from the spin.

I scanned the instruments, and the airspeed indicator showed forty knots at the bottom of the case. We were too slow. "Hos, watch the airspeed," I noted.

Immediately the aircraft fell off into a secondary spin before Hos could push the nose over. This time the spin went to the right. Now we were headed straight for the ground in a spiraling turn. We both fought the controls and managed to stop the spin a second time, but the Liberator was screaming toward the ground. The airspeed was over the "red line" now.

"Airspeed 300 knots," Hos said in a frantic voice.

"Pompeo, open the bomb bay doors," I yelled, hoping the extra drag would slow us down.

"*Bang.*"

"What was that?" Hos asked, startled while still fighting the controls. "It sounded like it came from the tail."

Suddenly, the aircraft whipped into a nose-up attitude, stalled, and fell into a third spin. I could hear Seibert and Wenz screaming in the back as we tried helplessly to control the plane.

Hos gave up and yelled, "Bail out! Bail out!"

I reached over, hit the red bailout button, and then returned to the controls to help Hos. I could hear Wenz and Seibert putting their parachutes on from the back.

Hos hit the microphone, "Leon, you and Pompeo get out. I'll hold it!"

I didn't wait for another second. Scrambling out of my seat, I crawled aft as Pompeo jumped out the bomb bay doors. I threw off my mittens, grabbed a parachute, and strapped it on. I could see the trees through the bomb bay doors getting larger. God, I didn't want to die. With one last glance, I saw Hos in the radio compartment, and then I jumped.

The deadly cold air hit me like a ton of bricks. As I descended in my chute, I spotted one other cute that was above me. It had to be Hos, I thought to myself.

The B-24 continued to spin until it impacted the side of a mountain and exploded into a massive fireball. Hos disappeared on the other side of the ridge.

Checking the ground below me, I picked out a landing spot, but I was at the mercy of the wind. I hit the steep side of the mountain hard and crumpled to the ground. On my back, I could see burning aircraft on the slope above me.

I waited a few seconds, got up, and yelled, "Hos! Wenz! Seibert!" But there was no reply. I cried out a couple more times, but no one answered. I was alone in a God-forsaken land.

I attempted to hike up the mountain to the crash site but was unable because of the steep grade and deep snow. My training taught me that my best bet was to stay with the wreck, but I couldn't get to it. I didn't know what to do, and I knew my choices now would be life-and-death decisions for me.

I was in trouble. I had no food, sleeping bag, or weapons and left my damn mittens in the aircraft. I knew the folks at Ladd had no idea where we were.

Resting briefly, I thoroughly checked my body to ensure I had no injuries. Everything felt fine except for some stiffness in my arms and legs. I didn't know if that was from the parachute or the icy cold conditions outside. I had on my new experimental down-filled flight suit, a Boy Scout knife, two books of matches, a letter from my father, and my parachute.

Figuring there was no chance of a rescue team finding me before I died of exposure or starvation, I decided to set out to find shelter.

I proceeded slowly down to a stream. At about four o'clock, when it got too dark to go any further, I stopped and made camp. I quickly gathered some small twigs and lit a fire. It took me four of my forty matches and my father's letter to get it started. After getting the fire going, I wrapped myself in my parachute and tried to sleep, moving as close to the fire as possible. Before falling asleep, I looked up the mountain and noticed the glow of my aircraft still burning against the Alaskan sunset.

On several occasions during the night, I dozed in and out of consciousness only to find my parachute on fire. The fire did little against the blistering night wind. I was shivering to death.

In the morning, I got up and decided not to try and make it up the mountain again. It was just too steep. My best chance was to find help down in the valley. I felt confident I could find civilization if I continued to work my way down the river. I trudged through the hip-high snow with great difficulty as my frostbitten hands started to bleed. Once, I tried to crawl over an icy boulder only to get halfway up and then slide back down. I was frozen from head to toe.

I spent another restless night wrapped in nothing but my parachute. That night I couldn't start a fire and just shivered, trying to stay awake. I knew if I fell asleep, I would be dead by morning.

On the third day, hunger pains hit my stomach. My body was slowing down due to a lack of sleep and food. I decided not to travel down the mountain anymore and wait for help. This decision almost cost me my life.

I camped in the same spot I had stayed the night before. I tried several vain attempts to kill some tree squirrels. I threw whatever I could find in the snow at them but had no luck. Instead, I settled for some snow and frozen moss, which I couldn't swallow, so I just nibbled on it.

The next day nearly passed before I remembered it was Christmas Day. The thought of my family eating Christmas dinner aggravated my hunger. I stayed in place a few more nights before I realized rescue would not be imminent. The cold was murderous, and combined with no food intake; my strength was being sapped from my body. I knew I had to move, or else I would die.

I spent the seventh night in my makeshift camp. That night I watched a spectacular display of the northern lights while I made plans to move out early the next day. No more waiting for something to happen. I had to take matters into my own hands.

The following day was bitterly cold but clear. My thinking was fuzzy, and I decided to head west and try to find the Alaskan-Canadian highway instead of going downstream. I calculated the highway was about two hundred miles away. This decision again nearly cost me my life.

I stumbled and crawled up the western slope of the river valley, losing my direction. At midday, I could still see the camp I had left earlier that morning. Exhausted and defeated, I sat down on some rocks and stared at my crooked path. I realized I couldn't make the two hundred miles to the Alcan Highway. I returned to my original camp and decided to move downriver the following day.

On the ninth day, I followed the river downstream, hoping to find a settlement or camp around the next bend. Incredibly, at dusk, I saw a man-made structure. It was a tent standing high above the ground on tall poles. The Alaskans called it a cache. My heart raced as I ran for the cache in the gathering of darkness. As I approached, I saw a small cabin and entered. It was large enough to hold a bed, table, and small wooden stove. Smiling to myself, I thought things were starting to look up.

I tore open several sacks on the table and found the fixings for hot chocolate and bags of dried fruit. I started a fire and melted a pan of snow. Soon, I was drinking hot cocoa and stuffing myself with raisins. I felt great, considering the circumstances.

Later, I found a ladder next to a tree. I climbed up the ladder to a little storage bin containing a variety of things, including tents, tarps, ropes, tools, and lanterns. I heaved the frozen tents into the cabin and laid them on the bunk. Wrapping myself up in my parachute inside the tents, I fell asleep. It was my first real sleep since bailing out of my aircraft.

The following day, I had another breakfast of raisins and hot chocolate. I stuffed my pockets with raisins and set out downstream to find a village.

Moving downstream all day and into the night, I found nothing. I wondered how such a well-stocked cabin could be so far away from a town. By midnight, I realized I was in serious trouble again. I estimated the temperature to be -50 degrees. My feet and hands were numb. I couldn't even move my fingers to strike a match. I had to make it back upriver to the cabin or I wouldn't make it.

I retraced my steps, drifting in and out of consciousness. At times, I would wake to wander away from the stream bed. I finally returned to the cabin near noon on New Year's Day. I lit a fire and then slept hard for the next two days.

On the twelfth day, I awoke rested. I was tired of raisins and hot chocolate. I returned to the cache to see if there was anything else to eat. In the daylight, I found a couple of burlap sacks full of flour, jerky, beans, dried soup vegetables, tea, lard, rice, and other foodstuffs. There was even clothing to include fur mittens! Still, further back in the cache, I found a rifle and some ammunition. The owner's name was on the side of one of the crates of supplies. The label read, "Phil Brail, Woodchopper, Alaska."

For the next week, I settled into domestic life. I concentrated on treating my frostbite and rebuilding my strength. I mended my clothes and made inventories. I even found a four-year-old calendar and kept track of the days by punching holes on each day with a nail. One evening, I accidentally knocked the calendar off the wall. As the calendar hit the floor, it fell open to a map of Alaska. I was ecstatic! I studied the map for several nights before seeing a town called Woodchopper. It was not until then that I realized Woodchopper was where Phil Brail lived, not what he did for a living.

The map was as much a lifesaver as the food and the cabin itself. Eventually, I determined I was on a tributary of the Yukon River, probably the Charley River. I also realized that I was still far from Woodchopper if I was on the Charley River.

I decided to make an exploratory trip downstream again. This time, I would better equip myself for the journey. I was in much better physical condition than the first time I made the trip. I made a backpack from my parachute and carried the rifle.

On 20 January, I headed out. On the first day out, I discovered a second cabin and a derelict canoe. On the second day, I found yet another place further downstream. I found some old mail in this cabin, again addressed to Woodchopper, Alaska. I also found a sleeping bag that I could use. No more wrapping myself up in my parachute to keep warm.

The next day I continued. On this day, I erroneously concluded I was nearing the Yukon River and returned to Phil Brail's cabin. Walking back upstream, I estimated I would need a two-week food supply to make it to Woodchopper. I also decided to wait a few more weeks until the weather improved.

The next several weeks were relatively routine. I hunted squirrels and ptarmigan. Daily, I chopped a hole in the ice for fresh water. I was living the very kind of life Phil Brail would have lived if he were there.

I started to get depressed as my thoughts were of my family. I realized my parents must have given me up for dead.

Another week passed, and I decided not to wait any longer. My ammunition was running low, and I heard the river ice crack several times, making walking on it dangerous. My strength had returned, and I felt up for the ordeal. I made a sled from some boards and an old washtub. I packed it with an estimated two-week supply of provisions and readied myself for the trip that would either save my life or end it. This was my last chance.

On 12 February 1944, I closed the door to Phil Brail's cabin for the last time. I laboriously lugged the crude sled through the snow, sometimes hip-deep. The sled was much harder to pull than I had figured. I couldn't, however, carry the two week's worth of supplies any other way, so I slowly made my way downriver.

One day I put my foot through some thin ice. My mukluk was frozen stiff within a few minutes, but my feet stayed dry. Several days later, I nearly lost my life again. I fell through the ice and stood armpit-deep in the icy Charley River. Scrambling up the snow-covered bank, I had minutes to live. I reacted quickly. While trembling uncontrollably, I started a fire and stripped down to my waist. I dried my upper body garments while stomping around in my frozen mukluks and trousers. Several miserable hours later, I donned my upper garments and stripped off my frozen lower garments.

The next day, I moved downriver again. On the 15th day of my trek from the Brail cabin, I found another deserted cabin. In it was a small supply of food. I stayed there for three days before striking out for the Yukon River. During those last weeks of winter, the temperature dropped to 25 degrees below freezing. The mucus in my nostrils froze when I inhaled sharply.

Finally, the temperature warmed slightly, and I could hear the ice cracking again. One day, the sled fell through while I was walking on the ice. Without the supplies on that sled, I knew I would never survive. I waded into the hip-deep water to recover my supplies and save the sled. I again had to stand naked before a fire while my clothes dried. I decided to leave the cumbersome sled and proceeded with only my backpack and rifle. It took another eight days to finally reach the Yukon River.

The next day, I found a dog sled trail and followed it until I found a cabin with smoke pouring out the chimney. I saw some clothes hanging on a clothesline. I could hear the sounds of dogs and children and the smell of hot food. As I approached the cabin, a startled gentleman stepped from the door.

"Hello there," he said. "You look lost?"

"I have been," I replied. "My name is Leon Crane, and I bailed out of a B-24."

Shaking my hand, he said, "Hi, I'm Albert Ames. Nice to meet you. Why don't you come into the cabin and warm up."

As he opened the door, Albert hollered inside, "Neena, we have some company." Turning to me, he said, "This is my wife, Neena."

I shook her hand and met Albert's three small children. After sitting down, I told Albert and Neena my incredible story and then explained how I had walked a hundred and twenty miles down Charley River. At first, I didn't think they believed me. Then Albert told me I was still thirty miles from Woodchopper. He also told me I was two hundred and fifty miles from Ladd Field.

"I tell you what," Albert said, standing, "tomorrow I'll give you a ride to Woodchopper on my dogsled."

"That would be great," I replied with relief.

The next day we arrived at Woodchopper. I sent a wireless message to a Wein Airline's bush pilot on his way to Circle, a village forty miles further downstream. I also sent two telegrams, one to my family and one to Ladd Field.

Before leaving Woodchopper, I also had the chance to meet Phil Brail. I couldn't thank him enough for keeping his cabin supplied. He told me that was the law in Alaska in case people became stranded during the winter. I offered to repay him for the supplies I took, but he declined.

Later that day, I was in the air headed for Ladd Field.

Approaching the base, bush pilot Bob Rice radioed, "Ladd Field, this is Wein Airlines requesting permission to land?"

"Wein Airlines, this is Ladd Field; state the reason for the request?"

Bob glanced at me and smirked as he replied, "Well, you're not going to believe this. I have one of your B-24 pilots onboard, Lt. Leon Crane."

After a few moments of silence, the operator asked, "Is he alive or dead?"

When we landed, the word of my arrival quickly spread. A small group of my friends met me at the airplane. People kept telling me, "I can't believe you're alive. I can't believe it."

As I walked into Base Operations, memories of my crew hit me. Eighty-four days ago, we had taken off from Ladd Field. Tears came to my eyes. Throughout the ordeal, I never cried, and now I couldn't stop.

They took me to the flight surgeon's office for a checkup. The Doctors said I was in great shape—I had even gained a little weight during my ordeal.

The next day the Base Commander gave me a big reunion with everybody on base invited. Following that, the commander arranged a personal phone call for me back to the lower States. I was able to speak to my parents and assure them that reports of my death were greatly exaggerated. Afterward, I headed for the PX and drank a large chocolate malt.

The next day, I boarded a B-24 and led the rescue team to the crash site. Within a week, ground parties found the remains of 1st Lt. Seibert and Sergeant Wenz in the aircraft. They were unable to get out of the spinning plane. They never found Master Sergeant Pompeo or Captain Hoskins.

CHAPTER 12

CW2 Daniel R. Smee and CW4 Franklin C. Harrison
AH-64 Apache

In our second story on survival, Daniel Smee, a former Army Ranger, puts his previous experience to work in helping his crew out of a bad situation. These two men would have been in serious trouble without CW2 Smee's extensive mountain training.

* * *

"Chalk 3 has sight on 2," I called over the radio, weaving around another snow-capped peak.

"Stay two hundred yards back," Lead replied.

"Roger," I responded.

The night reconnaissance mission through the mountains was anything but boring. I strained to keep sight of Chalk 2 around each bend in our four-ship staggered formation.

"Yeehaw," my backseater, CW4 Frank Harrison, cried out. "I can't believe the government pays me to do this."

Exhilaration ran through his blood as it did mine. The last thirty minutes had been one of the greatest sorties of our lives.

"Chalk flight, this is lead," the old major said. "Return to base, mission accomplished."

"Two . . . Three . . . Four," came the reply's over the radio.

Pulling around a peak, I began a hundred-and-eighty-degree turn back to the base. Suddenly, out of nowhere, a white wall of snow was in front of me.

"What the hell?" I yelled.

Within seconds I was smack dab in a massive snowstorm. I froze the stick in the same position and began to come on the instruments. My visual references outside were gone in a flash.

"Dan, get us out of here," Frank screamed at me.

I instantly increased the power and pulled on the collective to gain altitude.

"*Baaaam!*"

I could vaguely hear metal crashing against metal and the rotor disintegrating. The sudden impact jarred all thoughts from my head as I slammed forward into the Optical Relay Tube. My helmet saved me from a bone-crushing experience.

Slumped over, I could hear the engines' low hum as the blades beat themselves to death as we hit the ground. I crouched down as low as I could to avoid any blades that might come through the cockpit. I could hear fuel escaping from our ruptured auxiliary tank mounted on the right wing.

Then the helicopter stopped rocking from side to side. My first thought was I had made it. It took me a moment to realize we had impacted the top of a mountain.

"Frank?" I called out.

No answer.

Then the engines began to wind down. Frank must have shut them down, I thought to myself. That was a good sign.

Glancing backward, I saw the mic cord from my helmet had come unplugged. That would count as to why Frank was not answering me. Leaning back, I plugged the comm cord back in.

"Frank?" I asked.

Still no answer.

As the rotors stopped, I looked upwards. A huge hole appeared where our canopy was just seconds ago. Disconnecting my lap belt, I struggled out of my seat and pulled myself through the hole.

Falling five feet straight to the ground, I lay there for a minute with my face buried in the snow. I mentally checked all my body parts to ensure everything was connected. Feeling satisfied, I slowly got up and saw Frank coming around the nose of the chopper.

"Let's get out of here," he yelled. "She still could blow."

That was all the encouragement I needed as we hurriedly moved twenty-five feet from the smoking helicopter.

My adrenaline and heart were racing in high gear. "Frank, are you okay?" I asked in-between breaths.

"I think I broke my left arm," he said, pulling up his sleeve. A large black and blue bruise had already set in, but all the bones appeared in their original location. "How about you?" he asked.

I checked the entire length of my body. Tiny trickles of blood dripped off my fingertips. "Just a small cut on my right arm," I said. "We were pretty damn lucky, I'd say."

The helicopter continued to smoke through the blowing snow. The wind drove cold air through my flight suit at over twenty miles per hour. All of my gear was still back in the chopper.

I stood there watching the smoke for a few minutes and said, "I'm going back for my parka and sleeping bag."

"You think it's safe to go back?" Frank responded.

"If it were going to blow, it would have by now," I said, moving cautiously toward the craft. I checked to ensure there were no flames hidden within the smoke.

Leaning through the large hole, I hoisted out my oversized Gortex parka and the sleeping bag I had stowed behind the seat. Years earlier, I started packing a sleeping bag in case we ever had an emergency and had to spend the night out. That mindset was paying off now.

Blinding snow whipped around as I threw my heavy parka on. Instantly, I felt better from the warmth of the oversized coat. Then, out of nowhere, I heard the low hum of a helicopter circling to the south.

Frank heard the same thing and said, "Do you have your survival radio?"

"Yea," I said quickly, pulling it from my vest and turning it on. "Chalk flight, this is Chalk 3. Do you copy?"

No answer.

"It must be the storm," Frank hollered over the wind.

"Let me try the beacon mode," as I switched channels on the portable PRC-90 radio.

Still no reply.

"Well, there is no way they're going to be able to rescue us in this storm," I said, looking over the landscape. "There is no telling how long it will last."

"I say we climb down the mountain where the wind is not blowing as much," Frank suggested.

"I concur," I said, picking up my survival gear.

We walked over to the mountain's edge and looked down the valley floor. Both of us were mesmerized by the sheer steepness of the slope. I estimated the valley floor to be over seven hundred feet below us.

"Well, you're the former Army Ranger instructor," Frank said. "How the hell do we get down there?"

"Very slowly," I replied. "You got your flashlight?"

"I got two," he stated.

"Just shine it in front of me," I said, heaving my sleeping bag twenty feet below a ridge. "I'll lead."

"That's fine with me," Frank replied.

I grabbed some glove inserts from my leg pocket and put them on underneath my Nomex gloves.

I started down slowly, ensuring every foothold was secure before taking another. The terrain was steeper than I initially thought, and the wet snow made the rocks slippery. Gradually, I made my way to the first ledge.

"Throw me your sleeping bag," I yelled.

Frank heaved his bag at me. I caught it while almost losing my footing.

"Okay, you're next," I said. "I'll shine my flashlight on the rocks."

As Frank started down, I could feel the cold, wet snow getting under my parka. We needed to get down fast before hypothermia set in, but one misstep would mean a broken ankle or, worse, our lives.

Five minutes later, Frank made it to the ledge. We repeated the same process as we made our way down the mountain.

At the halfway point, I asked, "Frank how are you doing?"

"Fine, except for my fingers and toes," he said. "They're frozen."

Trying to move my extremities, I replied, "Mine too. Let's stop here and warm up before going on."

Frank took his gloves off and wrung the water out of them. I did the same. Then we both placed our hands inside our parkas until we could move our fingers freely.

"We don't have much further to go," I said, hoping to encourage Frank.

"I'm going to try another radio call; Frank said, "Chalk flight, this is Chalk 3 down and all right. Do you copy?"

Still no answer.

Frank looked at me, shaking his head, "I guess we keep going on."

A few ridges later, we came upon a twenty-five-foot drop-off. It was a real kick in the chest. "Crap!" I said out loud.

Glancing back up the mountain, "We'll, I don't think we can go back up."

"And we can't go down either," Frank added.

I surveyed the slope around us. It was too steep to set up our sleeping bags. They would slide off the edge with us in them.

"What do we do now?" Frank asked desperately. "I can't believe we survived a crash and then got stuck on the side of this mountain."

My mind could only think of one thing. "Have you ever seen the movie *Alive*?" I asked, chuckling.

"You mean the one where they crashed on a mountain and resorted to cannibalism?" he asked inquisitively, "Yea. Yeah, I saw it," Frank said. "Why you're not planning on eating me, are you?"

Smiling, I replied, "Not unless we don't make it down."

Frank didn't laugh. Instead, he reassessed the situation and said, "I can make it."

"If we move over there," I said, pointing to my left. "We can hang over the ledge, and the drop is only about seven feet."

"Are you sure. . . ." Frank started to say.

I threw my sleeping bag over the ledge before Frank could finish his sentence. Now we were committed.

Moving gradually along the sidewall until the drop narrowed, I hung onto the edge. Dangling my feet over the side, I let go and fell to the ground. Excruciating pain jaunted up from my frozen feet to my spine, but I was able to keep my balance. "Your turn," I yelled, swallowing hard.

Frank threw his bag to me and followed the same footsteps as I lit his way with the flashlight. I cushioned his fall as he jumped from the edge. It took Frank only a few minutes to make it down to the ledge, but it seemed like an hour. I could tell Frank was physically drained.

The terrain shallowed out as we picked ourselves up, and we made our way to a small streambed and followed it down to the valley floor.

Checking my watch; it had been two hours since we crashed.

The snow was blowing harder than ever in the narrow ravine. Both of us were soaking wet and frozen stiff. That was it, I told myself. We weren't going any farther.

"This is as good of a campsite as any," I directed. "We need to get a fire going and get out of these clothes."

Frank didn't respond as he stood there shivering.

"Why don't you gather some sagebrush, and I'll survey the area for a possible landing site for the rescue aircraft," I said.

"Okay," Frank replied as his teeth chattered in the bitter wind.

After a quick check, I found several sites to accommodate a helicopter safely. Trudging my way back to Frank, he had a small pile of twigs and some paper from his kneeboard crumpled up beside him.

"Did you find any matches?" I asked.

"They're in my survival vest, but my hands are too frozen to undo the zipper," he said.

I reached over and helped him with the zipper and snagged two packs of matches. I went through both packs trying to light the paper. None of the matches would ignite. They were all soaked from the wet snow.

"Hum. Let's try the emergency firestarter kit," I said.

Frank handed me the kit, and I gave it a try. It didn't work either, as the wind blew the flame out before it had a chance. I then tried the magnesium firestarter. Giving it a couple of swipes, it ignited, but the paper and wood were too wet to burn.

"Frank, do you still smoke?" I asked.

Shaking his head, "No, I gave it up three months ago."

"I don't imagine you still carry your lighter?" I inquired.

"No," he replied.

Suddenly we could hear the distinct sound of a helicopter overhead. We both stared into the night sky, hoping to see the craft.

"Rescue, this is Chalk 3. Do you copy?" I screamed into the transmitter.

Nothing but static.

The low rhythmic sound grew louder.

"Frank, get your flashlights and point them toward the chopper," I directed.

He instantly waved both flashlights back and forth as the bottom side of an Air Force UH-60 came into view.

The valley lit up like Christmas when they flipped on their landing lights. As the chopper settled to the ground, we grabbed our sleeping bags and headed toward them.

The door swung open, and a pararescueman jumped out to greet us. "Are you guys hurt?" he asked.

"Just frozen," I replied.

"We searched for you on top and saw sparks down here."

Frank and I looked at each other. We couldn't start a fire, but at least the rescue craft could see we were trying.

According to my watch, it had been two and a half hours since we crashed. It was the coldest and wettest two-and-a-half hours of my life.

RESCUE

"Risking one's life so others may live."

Every military pilot will always respond to a call to rescue individuals caught in dangerous predicaments. In some units, that is their sole peacetime mission. I hold any military pilot in rescue operations with the highest regard. Putting your life on the line to save another individual brings out the best in an aviator. Whether on the Atlantic's high seas or the cold, rugged terrain of Alaska, military pilots have answered the call to rescue.

A military pilot with more than ten years in the service has most likely had the opportunity to assist in a rescue. Numerous pilots begged to take the mission. It was not for fame and glory but for the necessity of the situation.

Rescue pilots hold a true honor in United States military history.

CHAPTER 13

Anonymous

C-9A Nightingale

This story deeply touched me. It was written anonymously and given to a military magazine. It is humbling to see someone not want to take credit for their remarkable handling of multiple emergencies during the rescue of burn victims.

* * *

"Honey, are you ready to go to bed yet?" my wife Priscilla asked.

"Yea, it's been a long day," I replied.

It was a warm Tuesday night, and I was at home sitting on alert for my C-9 Air Evacuation Squadron at Scott Air Force Base, Illinois. It was a great twenty-four-hour duty unless you got the dreaded phone call. The time home gave me some quality time with my family and to catch up on some chores.

"Just stay near a phone in case we activate your crew," my Operations Officer said before leaving the squadron.

I glanced at my alarm clock before I hit the bed. It read 10:45 p.m. I couldn't wait to get a good night's sleep. All my chores had worn me out more than I thought. "Good night, sweetheart," I said and closed my eyes.

"Goodnight," she responded.

The next thing I remember, I was in a deep dark dream in some faraway place. Bells were ringing everywhere as somebody was shaking my arm. They were screaming at me, but I couldn't understand what they said.

Suddenly, my eyes opened as my wife pushed me out of bed.

"Get the phone before it stops ringing," she said.

I could hear the ringing now, separating reality from my dream. I sat up and looked at my new digital clock, which read 1:01 a.m. As I reached for the phone, it finally dawned on me that I was still on alert.

"Hello," I responded in a groggy voice.

"Captain, this is the duty officer at Scott," the voice said professionally. "Your crew is being activated for an urgent mission to Casper, Wyoming."

"What's the deal?" I asked, still groggy.

"A family has been severely burned, and we need you to transport them to the Burn Center at Brooks Medical Center in San Antonio, Texas."

"Okay, I'll be in there as fast as I can," I replied, hanging up the phone.

"Honey, what's wrong?" Priscilla asked.

"Ah, some people got burned in Wyoming," I said calmly. "I have to go and pick them up and take them to San Antonio."

"Is it serious?" she asked.

"I don't know, but don't worry, I'll be fine," I said, jumping out of bed. "Just go back to sleep."

I threw my flight suit on and was out the door in ten minutes. I headed to the squadron as my mind ran through all the scenarios for burn victims and what considerations my crew would need to take.

At the squadron, people were scrambling in all directions. It was like a Chinese fire drill.

"Captain," echoed a husky voice around the corner.

"Hey Dave, how's it going?" I replied as my co-pilot walked up to me.

"Busy," he said, "but it's always like this when they launch an Air Evac Urgent sortie."

"Is the rest of our crew in yet?" I inquired.

"Most of them are. We're just waiting on the docs and nurses," he replied.

"All right," I said. "Let's check the weather and get a flight plan filed."

Within thirty minutes, I had completed my checklist and sat in the cockpit, ready to start the engines. It was relatively straightforward for us to fly the plane and transport the injured to the hospital. The back end of the plane was a different story. Five doctors, nurses, and medical technicians pushed equipment into place as my load operator strapped everything down. The entire back end of our C-9 was loaded with every life-saving medical device a person could think of.

"Can you believe the number of people we're taking?" Dave said, strapping into the right seat.

"I know," I responded. "I've never taken more than one doctor and a few nurses before. These people must be in pretty bad shape."

"I just hope we can get there in time," Dave replied sympathetically.

I nodded my head and switched the radio to ground frequency. "Ground Control, Rescue 10 will be ready for takeoff in ten minutes."

"Copy Rescue 10. Contact tower when ready," they replied.

We were airborne precisely ten minutes later, heading west toward Casper. Turning to my navigator I said, "Jim, find out what you can on these burn victims?"

"Roger," Jim replied said as he got on the HF radio and hooked up to a phone patch to the hospital in Casper. A few minutes later, he said, "Apparently, a mom, dad, and four kids were out on the range branding cattle. They were all gathered around a butane burner, which blew up, severely injuring all six."

"All of them are burned?" I asked in a surprised voice.

"Yes, sir," he fired back. "They have two civilian helicopters that will bring them to the airport to meet us."

"Okay, Dave, let's keep our speed up as fast as possible," I said. "I don't want to delay their recovery because of us."

"We're at .80 Mach," Dave affirmed.

The trip to Casper was uneventful as we landed ahead of our flight plan time. I shut the engines down, and two minutes later, the helicopters arrived with the family.

As the medical technicians transferred the patients from the helicopters to our plane, Dave and I ran into base operations to check the weather.

Stepping up to the counter, a tall man handed me a filled-out weather sheet and asked, "Rescue 10 flight?"

Impressed by his quickness, I replied, "Yes."

"You're going to be heading into some isolated thunderstorm on the way to Kelly Air Force Base, but you should be able to maneuver your way around them."

"Are we going to need an alternate field?" I inquired.

He responded, "With the weather, they're calling right now; yes, sir, you will."

"Crap!" I said, staring at Dave. "Do we have enough fuel on board?"

"Just barely. We're legal, but we don't have any to spare," Dave said.

"We could put a few thousand pounds on, but that will take thirty minutes," I responded.

"Probably longer than that," the weatherman said, "the fuel truck has shut down for the night."

I briefly considered our situation and stated, "I don't want to wait. Let's go with what we got."

"Sounds good to me," Dave said as we left.

Dave and I returned to the airplane with the weather sheet in hand. The medical personnel were ready to go as I went up the stairs. The back end looked like a full-fledged hospital. There were IV tubes, wires to heart monitors, oxygen hoses, and stuff I had never seen before—all of it with one purpose. To keep these six people alive so we could get them to the Burn Center.

"Casper Tower, Rescue 10 is ready for takeoff," I said, keying the microphone.

"Rescue 10, you're cleared for immediate takeoff on any runway."

"Rescue 10 copies," I responded.

Lifting off, I settled into my seat for the two-hour ride to San Antonio.

Then Dave suddenly said, "Captain, our pressurization is surging." puzzled.

Glancing at the gauge, I could feel the pressure changing in my ears. "Try the manual system," I directed.

Dave flipped the yellow pressurization switch to manual. "It works better than the normal system but still has some surges."

"Keep your eye on the gauge," I responded as a flight nurse approached the cockpit.

"Hi, I'm the Medical Crew Director," she said pointedly. "The pressurization is not doing my patients any good in—"

Raising my hand to cut her off I said, "I know, ma'am, our primary system is not working, and we're on the backup system."

"Can't you fix it?" she asked.

"We're trying our best," I replied, using all my will to be polite.

Upset, she spun around and headed out of the cockpit.

Dave looked over and smiled at me. We were both on the same wavelength. I won't tell you how to do your job if you don't tell me how to do mine, I thought.

"Thunder boomers ahead," Dave said, pointing out the window into the night sky. Lightning crisscrossed back and forth, presenting an ominous show.

I zigzagged back and forth for the next hour, dodging the big ones. Then, the boomers became so thick; I couldn't do anything but take them head-on. As I entered the clouds, we started taking ice on the wing.

"Dave, make sure the engine anti-ice system is on," I directed.

"Already got it," he replied, tapping on the pressurization gauge, "but something's wrong with the—"

Just then, the cockpit lights blinked off and then on, and they began flickering.

"What the heck?" I said out loud with a puzzled look.

"Pressurization is surging in the manual position now," Dave yelled.

"Turn off the anti-ice," I ordered, thinking that maybe the anti-ice was causing the problem.

"One second," Dave replied, moving the switch back.

Instantly I could feel the pressure pounding on my ears as they popped a couple of times.

"Turn the anti-ice back on; that's not the problem," I said.

"Roger," he replied.

Looking at the radar, I noticed it was in the "test pattern." That wasn't right either. I wondered to myself, what the hell was going on with our instruments?

Dave continued trying to fix the pressurization but to no avail.

Then the cockpit lights went off for good. We grabbed our flashlights and turned them on to see the gauges. Our aircraft was falling apart right before my eyes.

"Denver Center, this is Rescue 10?" I stated.

"Rescue 10, Denver Center, go ahead."

"We've lost our radar and would like course headings around the heaviest thunderstorms," I asked.

"Rescue 10, I show the entire area to San Antonio covered with Category four activity. Also, all the airports in the San Antonio area, including Kelly, are below minimums due to heavy thunderstorms. I can't do much to help you through the thunderstorms; for now, turn left twenty degrees."

I turned the plane to the left, but the airplane shook violently in the updrafts. "Dave, how's the pressurization?"

"I can't get it fixed," he replied.

Flying the jet manually, I quickly did some fuel computations in my head while checking the map for a good alternate place to land.

"Jim, get the head doc up here," I ordered my nav.

A minute later, an older gentleman dressed in a white uniform stood beside me. "Listen, doc; I can't get us into Kelly Air Force base; it's too dangerous."

He looked straight into my eyes and dropped a bomb on me. "Captain, if we don't get these people to the Burn Center, the mother and one of the boys will be dead in two hours." Then he turned around and left.

God, what was I supposed to do now? I didn't have radar or cockpit lights, and our pressurization was messed up. If I continued to Kelly, I might end up killing everybody. If I diverted to an alternate field, two people would die.

"We got ice building up on the wings," Dave blurted out. "I don't think the anti-ice is working either."

"Great," I replied, shrugging my shoulders. "What else can go wrong?"

"Our fuel situation is not too good either," Dave responded to add to our misery. "We've used most of our holding reserves maneuvering around the thunderstorms."

Looking at my map, we could hold for no more than ten minutes, and then we'll have to find another place to go.

As we approached Kelly, I established us in a holding pattern at thirty-one thousand feet and switched over to tower frequency.

"Kelly Tower, Rescue 10 is coming in with sick passengers," I said.

"Rescue 10, Kelly is closed due to thunderstorms," they replied back.

"Kelly, we need to get in—" I stopped mid-sentence as my ears began popping.

"Cabin pressurization has quit," Dave screamed, "and is climbing at twenty-five hundred feet per minute."

I took a deep breath and said, "I'm starting a descent now." Pushing the yoke over, I began the emergency procedure for the loss of pressurization.

"Oxygen 100 percent," I yelled over the intercom.

"Oxygen set," everybody answered with.

"Throttles idle," I stated as I pulled them back. "Speed brakes extended."

"Extended," Dave responded.

We were in deep kimchi I thought. We're descended into thunderstorms with little fuel to a field below minimums and using a flashlight to see the gauges with six burned people in the back. I said a quick prayer and then got on the radio.

"Houston Center, Rescue 10 is now declaring an emergency," I said forcefully.

"Rescue 10, this is Houston Center," the voice replied. "We copy your emergency. Kelly is three hundred and three-quarters visibility and improving."

At last, some good news, I thought; "Jim, find out how the patients are doing?"

He quickly went to work without answering, talking to the head doctor in the back.

Ten seconds later, he replied, "They're doing okay; cabin altitude is leveling at twenty-one thousand."

I did my best to dodge the heavy lightning areas when we broke out of the clouds at nine thousand feet. Finally, things were coming together.

"Twenty minutes of fuel left," Dave hollered.

I had to work quickly. I couldn't afford to dodge any more thunderstorms. We wouldn't make it if I did.

Lining up on final, I lowered the gear and flew down on the Instrument Landing System. Everything had gone wrong on this flight. It was like we were trying to avoid the Grim Reaper.

"Gear down," I directed.

With his left hand, Dave lowered the landing gear.

We broke out of the clouds at three hundred feet with the runway dead ahead. It was the prettiest sight I had ever seen before.

Touching down, I could almost hear the silent cheers from all on board, including myself. It was a good feeling to be back on terra firma.

The ambulances from the burn center meet us at the ramp. After unloading the passengers, I sat back in the seat and thanked God for saving our lives. We had cheated death once again.

Five weeks later, I was flying another Air Evac mission through Kelly when a young man came to look at my airplane. It was common for kids to come out and want a tour of our jet. I showed him around, explaining the cockpit's different dials, gauges, and switches.

Most young men are interested only in the cockpit and what pilots do upfront. As we started to leave, the boy asked if he could look at the back end. I was happy to show him.

While walking to the rear of the plane, the boy told me a short story about how he and his Mom, Dad, two brothers, and sister had ridden on an airplane like this one after being burned on a cattle ranch in Wyoming. As the boy walked away with tears flowing down my eyes, I finally got enough courage to ask him how his family was doing.

He replied, "It's been tough, but we're all getting better."

CHAPTER 14

Major Michael G. Shook
H-60 Blackhawk

Sometimes in rescue operations, there is a reason they call in the military. In this story, the crew has to make one of the most daring rescues into a canyon with no room to maneuver and even less room for error.

* * *

"Mike, get the kids out of bed so we won't be late for church," my wife hollered from the kitchen.

"I'll be there in a second," I replied as the phone started ringing. "Hello."

"Is this Captain Mike Shook?" the soft-voiced man asked.

"Yes, it is," I replied.

"This is Sergeant Lowery from Base Operations. I have a phone patch to the Sheriff's department," the Sergeant replied. "Go ahead, you're connected."

"Captain Shook, this is Sheriff Jenkins. I'm sorry to bother you on a Sunday, but we are conducting a life-and-death recovery for several individuals stranded in Hell's Hole Canyon."

"All right," I said, listening intently.

"We don't have a helicopter equipped with a hoist, so I called your base. Can you come out and help us?" he inquired.

"No problem," I replied. "I'll assemble a crew, and we'll be airborne in ninety minutes."

"Thanks, I appreciate it," the Sheriff responded as he hung up the phone.

Rushing to base, I assembled a Supervisor of Flying (SOF) and a crew for the rescue operation. I quickly went through the briefing, mission planning, and preflight at the squadron. Everything was flowing smoothly, and ninety minutes later, we launched.

I sat in the left seat as the copilot, and Captain Randy Johnson was in the right as the Aircraft Commander.

Just after takeoff, the SOF called, "Rescue 56, I have confirmed there are three individuals stuck in the canyon."

"Do they have any rescue effort underway at this time?" I asked.

"Some rescue volunteers are trying to get them out by rope but aren't having any luck," he replied. "They've set up a base camp at the foot of the canyon and want you to land there first."

"Rescue 56 copies all," I said, checking the map while Randy flew. We were a hundred miles away from Hell's Hole Canyon.

"Mike, check the power requirements for the pickup?" Randy asked.

I quickly calculated the power needed for the recovery by using the outside air temperature and the altitude of the canyon.

"I calculate we should have a ten to fifteen percent power margin," I replied. "That should be more than enough."

"Okay, we'll recheck it later just to be safe," Randy said.

Forty minutes later, we were approaching the base camp. It was a beehive of activity. Sheriff vehicles, deputies, rescue volunteers, and a News Channel helicopter cluttered the large meadow.

I double-checked our power requirements again and reconfirmed the same numbers for the five thousand-foot canyons.

Hovering over the camp, Randy picked a safe place and landed. As our rotors came to a stop, a big rough, looking country Sheriff and another man approached us. "Hello," he said, sticking his hand out. "I'm Sheriff Jenkins, and this is Ted Vrable, one of our rescue volunteers."

"Hi, I'm Captain Mike Shook," I replied as I greeted both men.

"I want to send Ted with you to show you the way to Hell's Hole Canyon," Sheriff Jenkins directed.

"No problem," I responded. Pointing to the other helicopter, I said, "I need to make sure the News helicopter doesn't get in our way."

"I already thought of that and briefed them to stay a quarter mile from the rescue operation."

Turning around, I stated, "Great, let's go then," as I waved for Ted to follow me.

I cranked up the engines, and Randy and I were airborne again.

Ted vectored us down through the canyon. Within a minute, we were hovering over the site. Hell's Hole was one mile from the base and five hundred feet lower in altitude.

Randy flew a wide downwind to a long final approach from north to south, affording me time for a thorough site evaluation.

"Visual references look better on your side," Randy said. "Why don't you take the recovery?"

Taking the controls, I replied, "I have the aircraft."

The helicopter felt great in my hands as it purred through the controls.

Randy and I were fully qualified Night Tactical Instructors, so who was flying didn't matter. Today I was lucky since I had better features to reference from my side.

"Left scanner call out altitude," I yelled, hovering directly over the bowl.

"Two hundred and fifty feet," he fired back.

I was about fifty feet above the canyon ridgeline at this altitude, looking directly down the bowl. I had an excellent view of Hell's Hole from my vantage point.

The bowl was open on the north side. The south side of the Hole was off the nose of the helicopter and was downhill to a narrow bend in the canyon blocked by a wall of tall trees. A cliff wall formed the east and west sides.

"Do you see the survivors?" Randy asked.

Glancing out my side window, I spotted them. "Yea, they're in the center, stranded on a large rock," I replied.

Gradually, I started the descent. The canyon was tighter than I had initially thought. The surface was rugged and carpeted with scrub brush and large boulders the size of a house.

"There's no place to land if something goes wrong," I said, uneasy.

"Just concentrate on staying in the center," Randy replied. "We'll get a hundred feet above them and lower the cable."

"Scanners, how are we looking?" I asked.

"So far, so good," one of them responded.

I double-checked the power margin again while the scanners cleared me down. Gently, I lowered the helicopter to a hundred-foot hover directly over the survivors.

"Right scanner, you're cleared to send the rescue device down," I directed.

"Lowering the hoist now," he replied.

Hovering in the bowl and below the ridgeline, I thought about my wife enjoying a quiet Sunday morning, drinking coffee, and reading the Sunday newspaper. I was sure my entire crew would have also preferred to be with their wives. However, this was a life-and-death rescue, and they needed us.

"We got one coming up," the right scanner yelled over the intercom.

"Power looks good," Randy said.

"Left scanner; I feel pretty stable here," I said. "Help out the right if he needs it."

"Wilco."

"Engine instruments look fine," Randy responded.

I cross-checked my outside references to maintain my position. I noticed Ted staring outside, obviously enjoying the scenery.

"First one's inside—"

The noise level suddenly changed. Something was wrong.

"LOW ROTOR!" Randy screamed.

I quickly glanced at the tachometer. The RPM was deteriorating. Glancing outside at my references, we were descending.

"I'm losing it," I yelled.

"RPM still decreasing," Randy hollered.

In a split second, I had lost nearly forty feet. "We're going down," I screamed.

There was no place to land. My instincts told me to lower the collective, taking demand off the engine, but I knew this would increase my rate of descent and speed up an impact with the survivors directly beneath me.

I had to do something to preserve what little rotor RPM I had left. "Right, rudder," I said, screaming out loud.

Immediately the pitch flattened out, lessening the load on the main rotor. I applied cyclic control in the downhill direction just as the helicopter started to rotate around its vertical axis, moving us away from the survivors and towards the cliff wall.

"Clear left!" one scanner yelled.

"Clear, right!" the other scanner followed.

Slowly the rotor decay decreased after I applied the right rudder. I then tried a slight amount of up collective to break my descent rate. It didn't work. The rotor decayed further, and our descent increased. I applied more right rudder.

"Clear left!"

"Clear, right!" came from the scanner.

Randy hollered, "Watch the trees. You still have low RPM."

Losing altitude and rotating through a second turn, the trees along the cliff wall became blurred. I didn't have enough power to keep the helicopter airborne. We were going to impact the ground.

"Survivors are clear!" the left scanner called out.

I looked down over my left boot through the chin bubble and saw a boulder the size of a Volkswagen Bug. Descending, I applied cyclic away from the wall of trees and the cliff, stopping our lateral movement. I then applied left rudder to stop the rotation, aiming for the Volkswagen size rock. "We're going in!" I repeated.

The rotor deteriorated into the danger zone, increasing our rate of descent. At least I was able to keep the helicopter in a level attitude.

"Scanner, how's our landing spot?" Randy hollered.

"Looks good!" he screamed.

"Brace for impact," I yelled.

Suddenly, the main rotor blades hit the cliff wall. I heard a deafening "*Kaboom*" as the helicopter jolted severely to a sudden stop.

The force of the impact was tremendous. We hit level on a platform of rocks between two ponds at the base of the cliff wall. There was just enough room for the helicopter but not enough for the rotor blades. The blades bounced off the walls slicing into the trees, exploding into a million pieces.

Then another explosion rocked the right side of the chopper as a large fire engulfed the helicopter. The craft thrashed violently on the rocks from an imbalance to the rotor head.

"Egress! Egress! Egress!" Randy screamed.

Randy immediately jumped out of his seat and through the door with the right scanner in trial with a fire bottle.

I tried to move my legs, but pain rippled through my spine. My door was twisted and buckled from the impact, so I pulled myself hand-over-hand through a small opening of twisted steel to the left of my instrument panel.

Once clear of the burning helicopter, I fell head-first onto my back in the small pond below. Ted came tumbling out beside me. Looking up, I saw the left scanner was trapped. His right leg was pinned between the cabin door and the Volkswagen size rock.

I tried to help him but still couldn't move my legs. Fire from the number one engine blazed out of control above the left scanner's head.

"Ted, get the fire out," I directed.

Dazed, the Sheriff's rescue volunteer stood up in the water.

"Here," I said, tossing him my helmet.

Realizing what I wanted him to do, he immediately started using my helmet as a bucket to extinguish the fire. Within three minutes, Ted was able to put the fire out as Randy and the right scanner were fighting the blaze on the other side.

Once all the fire was extinguished, the three of them dislodged the scanner's leg and threw him into the water beside me.

"Mike, are you okay?" Randy asked.

"Yea, I think my back is broken," I said, feeling numb from my waist down. "Did all the survivors make it?"

"Yea, everybody's fine," Randy said. "Hell, they had a bird's eye view of our crash.

I rested my head on the rocks thanking God it was over, and we were all alive. Four hours later, another helicopter from my squadron transported my crew and me to Scottsdale Memorial Hospital.

CHAPTER 15

Major Chuck Foster and Captain Brett Hartnett
HH-60 Blackhawk

After major maintenance, every pilot is anxious about taking an aircraft into the air. In this story, there was no time to check out the helicopter before being called to duty. It takes a great crew to handle two challenging situations simultaneously.

* * *

The hot afternoon sun was starting to take its toll on me. Yawning, I said, "Third times a charm."

"I hope so," my copilot Captain Brett Hartnett replied. Turning my head toward the back of the helicopter, I hollered, "Crew chiefs, are you ready to go again?"

"Yes sir, we're ready," one fired back.

"Okay, buckle up," I yelled over the engine noise. "Here we go again." Pushing the power up, I gradually pulled back on the collective as the chopper rose.

We had spent most of the afternoon finding problems with our helicopter. Twice after getting airborne, the crew chiefs found excessive vibrations coming from the rotor heads, and we had to sit down and fix the problem.

"Departure control, Jolly 55 is with you again," Brett said.

"Jolly 55," the voice replied abruptly. "Can you respond to an aircraft emergency and head down to Chickaloon Flats?"

Brett and I stared at each other as we were taken off guard by the call.

Before I could respond, the controller said, "We have a report of a crash in that area."

"Standby," I responded.

The standby call must have been perceived as a tacit "Yes" because the controller came back and said, "There's an aircraft orbiting overhead at four thousand feet. I can give you a heading if you want."

The copilot and I were still studying each other. There was no doubt we wanted to respond, but I had a few mental hurdles to jump through first. I could only imagine how it might be read in a mishap report if we deviated from our planned aircraft checkout. Would my peers think it a wise move; I wondered to myself.

The persistent controller would not let up, and stated, "Jolly 55, the crashed aircraft is on fire. Maybe you can see the smoke from your position."

I knew Brett from many flights together and I told him, "You have the aircraft."

"Roger, I have the aircraft," he replied. "Departure, 55 will respond. Please advise for an initial heading."

"Heading 180, and thanks, guys," the controller responded.

Brett yelled, "Right turn!" as he sharply banked the helicopter to the south.

I quickly took over all the radios and switched to Approach Control's frequency, thus relieving Brett from everything but flying the helicopter.

"Approach, Jolly 55 is heading southbound to an emergency," I said.

"Jolly 55, radar contact," she responded. "The accident is nine miles off your nose."

Haze sloped across the horizon, cluttering our forward vision. I strained to see through the smoke in the distance but couldn't. It didn't matter, I thought; we'd be there in less than five minutes traveling at a hundred and fifty knots.

"Engineer, do we have any medical equipment on board?" I inquired.

"No sir, only test equipment," he replied.

There was no time to go back for the equipment, I thought. Besides, it didn't matter; I had no clue what equipment a survivor of an airplane crash would need.

Brett said, "Approach, can you vector any aircraft out of the way between our positions?"

"55, we're doing that now," she replied.

"Major Foster, we'll need to shut the radar off before the rescue," the flight engineer hollered through the intercom.

"Good idea," I replied, hitting the switch and disabling our radar. The radar emitted harmful signals fifteen feet in front of the helicopter. The last thing I wanted to do was sterilize somebody after we saved them.

I began to feel in the grove, but at the same time, I was worried we'd forgotten something. My biggest problem was we were on a rescue mission in a helicopter that I hadn't been certified to fly yet.

The flight engineer tapped me on the shoulder and said, "All the test equipment is stowed."

"Thanks," I replied.

I hadn't thought about that either. Was there anything else I was missing? Here we were, en route for less than two minutes, and we'd made a dozen decisions and committed ourselves to a course of action. Did we think this through? It seemed so cut and dried, but we still needed to identify all the risks to this mission.

"Where is this going to rise up and bite us?" I asked the crew.

"Well, we are in a plane on a red 'X,'" one of the crew chiefs offered. The rest of the crew noted point.

"I just have two questions," I stated. "Crew chiefs, are you confident we won't fall out of the sky?"

"Yes!" they both replied together.

"Second, is everybody still a go on this?" I queried.

"Yes," everyone replied in unison again.

I was still not satisfied we were doing the right thing, "Approach, Jolly 55?"

"Go ahead," she responded.

"Are there any other rescue craft in the vicinity?" I inquired.

"No," she said; "you're it."

Case closed, I thought. It was us or nobody.

Nearing the crash, I began to see the fire. It was something out of a movie! The aircraft was engulfed in flames, but there was little smoke except for the mushroom cloud from the original flash. It hung overhead like a cloud of doom, but at the same time, it gave me the best indication that the winds would not be a problem on the landing.

"Jolly 55, this is Supercub 8LWT above," a man said. "Do you have me in sight?"

"55 has you in sight," I replied, looking through my ceiling window.

"Two guys made it out of the airplane before it caught fire," the Supercub pilot stated; "both are upwind of the wreckage."

"Jolly 55 copies. Thanks for your help," I responded.

I immediately spotted both men as we hovered overhead. One of the survivors looked like he was in shock, walking around in a daze. I could see his hands were black and burnt from the crash. The other man was on the ground about seventy-five feet from the fire. Even from the air, I could tell he was critically burned too.

"Brett, stay away from the dazed one," I directed. "I don't want him walking into our rotor."

"No problem," Brett replied.

I reached down and turned off Brett's access to the radios so he could hear only intercom transmissions. The flight engineer did the same. I didn't want any distractions for Brett as he prepared to land.

We surveyed the marshy ground below us for a suitable landing site. If we landed far from the crash, it would be hard to muck our way to and from the helicopter.

The flight engineer pointed to the right. "How about over there? It's a crosswind landing so we won't be downwind of the crash."

"I concur," Brett replied.

"All right, let's go for it," I said.

Brett rolled the helicopter to the right and hovered above the area. "How about right there off the nose?" Brett asked no one in particular.

The flight engineer answered, "That's fine," and then continued calling out altitude calls to Brett. He was essentially talking him down on the landing.

Brett lightly set the skids down on the marsh grass as the flight engineer yelled, "Request permission for the three of us to be cleared off?"

"You're cleared," I yelled as the engineer and the two crew chiefs jumped out the door.

Turning to me, Brett said, "I want to go too?"

"What!" I exclaimed.

"Maj, there's no way the three of them will be able to haul the two survivors back here through this muck," Brett answered.

I continued listening to his reasoning.

"Besides, the crew chiefs are unfamiliar with the rescue gear, and I am…"

"All right," I said reluctantly, cutting him off mid-sentence, "you're cleared off."

"Thanks," Brett said, squirming out of his harness and out the door in a couple of seconds.

I took the controls of the chopper. From inside the cockpit, I watched as the four crewmembers hurried to the survivors. One of the crew chiefs ran to the passenger with burned hands. Seeking to cool his skin in a nearby river, he had slipped down a steep, muddy embankment and disappeared from view. I could only hope the crew chief could get him back out of there.

The other three men headed for the other victim. I could tell he was in great pain and unable to sit up. He was black from head to toe and tore at his burned clothing to soothe the pain, but it wasn't helping.

I could see the flight engineer and Brett hollering back and forth at each other. After their brief exchange, they both ran back to the helicopter.

"What's up?" I screamed, looking back at the open door.

"We need the Stokes litter," Brett said. "This guy's in terrible shape."

The flight engineer grabbed a sleeping bag and rolled it out on the wire basket, providing more cushion for the survivor.

After a few minutes of shuffling their way back through the muck, they gently lifted the man into the litter. By his actions, I could tell he was screaming at the top of his lungs.

"Rescue, this is Jolly 55?" I said with no response. I tried again, but no one answered. I wanted dearly to tell them what was happening so they could tell us which hospital to go to, but they weren't hearing me for some reason.

Grabbing the map, I loaded the coordinates for three hospitals into the navigation system and selected Chickaloon General as my primary.

Taking a deep breath, I retraced everything for the flight to the hospital. Was I ready to go?

A minute later, covered knee-deep in mud, the flight engineer and Brett returned with the survivor in the Stokes litter.

"How is he?" I asked Brett.

"It's going to be close," he said. "He's got third-degree burns all over his body."

I shifted my focus back outside as the other crew chief began pushing the other survivor up a slippery embankment. Without the use of his hands, the survivor struggled haplessly. Finally, they made it back to the helicopter.

As the two survivors were strapped in, I increased power as Brett gave me a thumbs up.

"Everybody ready to go?" I yelled over the intercom

"Yes!" the flight engineer responded.

We were off after being on the ground for only a few minutes. This time I flew since I had reviewed the landing procedures for the hospital.

"Is everybody familiar with Chickaloon General?" I asked.

The flight engineer responded, "Yea, I've been there several times. It's a little tricky, but no big deal."

"Brett, get on the horn and talk to our command post. Tell them we're going to General," I directed.

"Roger," Brett said, keying up the radio.

"Maj, they have an air ambulance at General," the flight engineer said. "Maybe we can talk to them directly?"

"Good idea," I replied, motioning to Brett. "Give it a try."

Brett made several calls, but no one answered.

"Double check the freq," I told him.

"I did," he replied. "It's the right frequency."

"Well, don't worry about it; we're almost there," I said as the city's outskirts appeared off our nose.

"Command post, this is Jolly 55," Brett said.

"Jolly 55, go ahead," they replied.

"55's inbound to General. Can you call and tell them we have two burn victims and will be there in less than five minutes."

"Wilco," Command post responded.

I arrived at the hospital expecting to see a greeting party. There was none. Two helicopter pads were visible. One small landing pad was next to the emergency room doors, while the other was half a mile away. The closer one offered quicker access to care, but it was also the riskiest.

"I'm going for the closer pad," I said, looking for agreement.

Brett replied, "That would be my choice too."

"All right, Brett, you get the before-landing checklist while I set up the approach," I directed.

"Gear!" he yelled.

"Down and locked," I responded.

After completing the check, I was ready to go. Mindful of my ability to make a mistake, I added, "If I start to screw up, anybody can call a go-around. It won't take long to try again."

"Let's do it," Brett said, reassuring me and my abilities. "Seventy feet high," he stated.

I slowly lowered the collective, ensuring every move I made was precise.

"Fifty feet," Brett called out, then; "Ten."

Gently, the skids hit the pavement. "Okay, you're cleared off," I yelled.

As the crew chiefs and the flight engineer helped carry the two burn victims inside, I could see people peering out of the emergency room doors to see all the noise. Realizing an emergency was in progress; they quickly reappeared with a gurney.

I watched the two survivors disappear into the hospital as the crew returned to the helicopter. Glancing at my watch, I saw it had taken less than twenty minutes from when they notified us till we got the survivors to the hospital. It seemed like an eternity.

Looking back at the cabin, I yelled, "Good job, boys."

Everyone gave a thumbs up, and a couple of high-fives came from the crew chiefs. The cabin was a mess, and we were all bone tired.

Catching my breath, I added power as we lifted off for the home base. Before landing, we got our vibration readings. My aircraft was still out of limits and not qualified to fly on a routine mission.

MALFUNCTIONS

"Hours of pure boredom interrupted by moments of sheer terror"
Hours of pure boredom interrupted by moments of sheer terror is the only way to describe military flying. You see a movement on a gauge from the corner of your eye. You watch intently, knowing something is wrong. Then, all of a sudden, the fire light goes on, and your nice relaxing day becomes a nightmare.

The best professionals in the world maintain military aircraft. Most of the time, the enlisted crew that owns the plane treats it as a thoroughbred. They wash it, baby it, and put it to sleep at night.

A long-standing tradition in the military is for the pilot to salute the crew chief as they taxi the plane out. In a way, the gesture is to acknowledge all their hard work. Thank you for letting us borrow the aircraft for a little while. After all, the plane always goes back to maintenance. They own it and love it.

Malfunctions, however, are inevitable. How pilots treat those malfunctions determines the outcome. Training, skill, and teamwork exemplify success during an emergency. The US Air Force works painstakingly at these traits to ensure the best-trained aviators worldwide. A fact that has been proven many times on the battlefield and in peacetime.

CHAPTER 16

Captain Brian Udell
F-15E Strike Eagle

Brian Udell is one of only a handful of military aviators that have successfully ejected from an aircraft at over 780 miles per hour. All technical manuals for high-speed military jets state that you can expect severe bodily injury if ejecting over 700 miles per hour. Here is a story of a man who survived and continues to fly in the military today. Unbelievable.

***

The sun was setting on Seymour Johnson Air Force Base on April 18, 1995, when we took off. I was scheduled as part of a four-ship formation with three other F-15s. Tonight we would split into two groups and engage each other as simulated friendly and enemy forces—part of our routine training.

Within minutes after takeoff, our four-ship was over the Atlantic Ocean.

"Eagle 10 and 11 flight, give me a radar check?" I asked.

"Two's good . . . Three same. . . . Four's good," came the replies.

Darkness prevented a visual at night on the other aircraft in the fight. Radar was an absolute necessity to ensure our -15s didn't collide with each other. Without an operable radar, we would have to terminate and return to the base.

"Eagle flight split now," I said confidently on the radio.

"Eagle 11," replied the third ship as he and four peeled off my right wing.

I maneuvered toward the north with my wingman on my tail while the other two aircraft headed to the south.

Three minutes later, Captain Dennis White, my weapons systems officer in the back seat, said, "Radar contact, twenty miles apart."

That was my queue as I started a hard turn toward the other aircraft. It was the beginning of our jousting match to see who could win the aerial battle for the night.

During the turn, I glance at my heads-up display. It showed me in a 60-degree turn with my nose-tilted 10 degrees down and going 400 knots. We were level at 24,000 feet. Perfect, I thought to myself.

Before completing the turn, I started to hear the wind howling across the canopy. Something was wrong, I thought. At 400 knots, the wind didn't make that much noise. Usually, the howling came when we were accelerating through five hundred knots in the F-15.

"Dennis, do you hear that?" I inquired.

"Yea, it sounds like we're going supersonic," he replied.

Something was not right.

"I don't like this," I said out loud. I rechecked the heads-up display. All the gauges indicated normal.

"It sounds like we're heading straight for the ground," said Dennis.

"I know," I remarked as I flipped on the electronic attitude direction indicator. It took a second for the indicator to come alive. The gauge was a backup system to tell me if I was going up or down, left or right, or even upside down.

"Holy Crap!" We both screamed simultaneously.

The gauge read 600 knots or nearly 700 miles per hour. I rechecked the heads-up display. It still read 400 knots. I was baffled. I didn't know which set of instruments was telling me the truth.

Immediately, I started moving the stick back and forth to feel the airplane's response. The heads-up display stayed the same, but the electronic attitude indicator changed. That meant it was functioning correctly, and my heads-up display had malfunctioned.

"Lead, are you okay?" my wingman hollered.

I didn't have time to reply as Dennis yelled, "Brian, we're approaching 10,000 feet and descending fast."

We were screaming toward the earth like a giant lawn dart. I had to make a quick decision. The maximum speed for a safe ejection in the ACES II was 600 knots, and now we were well above that. But we would hit the ground if we didn't eject within seconds. With pitch-black skies and no horizon to work with, I ordered: "Bail out! Bail out! Bail out!"

Yanking my feet back in the stirrups and bracing myself, I pulled the handles at 6,000 feet. Due to the design of the ACES II ejection seat, Dennis left the aircraft first at 4,500 feet. I went second and saw the altimeter passing through 3,000 feet when I went up the rails. We were traveling straight down at 1,200 feet per second, faster than most rifle bullets.

The opening shock was horrendous as I was hurled through the supersonic shock waves. Instantly, I pulled my ripcord on my parachute at just under 1,000 feet.

Slowly descending, I felt as though a train had hit me. Somewhat getting my bearings, I went through my pre-programmed ejection checklist.

"Canopy," I said to myself. It was too dark to see anything as I glanced upward, and since it didn't feel like I was dropping like a rock, I figured it was okay. "Visor." At this time, I realized my helmet and oxygen mask had been completely ripped off my face. Even my earplugs were snatched out of my ears.

Glancing down at my arms, I could see both my gloves and watch had disappeared into the night. All my pens and flight suit patches were gone. My wallet and water bottle had blasted through the bottom of my G-suit pockets, even with the zippers still closed.

I could feel some pain, but I had no clue where it was coming from. My whole body hurt like hell. I then attempted to inflate my life preserver but found it was shredded by the windblast.

Finding my life raft cord, I started reeling in my life raft. During this process, I felt incredible pain coming from my left arm.

I knew immediately my arm was broken since it wouldn't work. I pulled the cord up with my right arm and bit the cord with my teeth to hold, then I would pull up some more cord again using my teeth. I hit the water like a rock.

I didn't see the water rushing up at me, but instantly I felt the bone-chilling coldness of the Atlantic Ocean. Coming up for air, I knew I had to get into my life raft, or else I would sink to the bottom without a life preserver.

Trying to dog paddle to the raft, I noticed my legs were not cooperating. Excruciating pain from my legs started to come up through my spine. I knew something was busted, but I could see through the water.

I had been trained in many different techniques to board the one-person life raft, but that was with four good limbs. Now the only limb that was working for me was my right arm.

With my arm wrapped over the edge, I tried as hard as possible to pull myself inside, but I couldn't get into the raft. I tried again and again but with the same results. I knew I couldn't hold onto the raft for too much longer. My strength was draining from my body.

Pausing, I looked up into the sky. "God, I need your help more than ever. Please help me get into this raft," I yelled into the dark moonless night.

After a few minutes, I mustered enough energy to try again. Somehow I managed to inch my way inside the raft. "Thank you, Lord," I cried out in joy.

Sitting in the rubber raft, I noticed my right leg was crooked out in front of me. From the knee down, it involuntarily dangled at a 90-degree angle over the right side of the raft. I almost freaked out. I had never seen a leg do that.

I grabbed my right leg and jerked it into the raft with my right arm. It flopped 180 degrees over my left leg. I adjusted it until the entire limb aligned in the same direction as my left leg. Then I noticed my left ankle was bent backward. I now understand why they wouldn't work when I was dog paddling in the water. Nothing was holding my legs together.

After I got my legs and left arm straightened out, I quickly checked the rest of my body for any deformities. I didn't find anything life-threatening problems other than my three broken limbs.

I wondered if I might go into shock while looking at my busted up limbs. I knew I had to treat myself quickly before I lost complete consciousness. Reaching into my emergency pack, I grabbed some water with my right arm and started guzzling it down as fast as possible.

The bone-chilling Atlantic wind made me hypothermic after chugging three containers of water. As I sat in frigid water, the waves crashed over the raft's side. I was frozen stiff, and now the cold bothered me more than my injuries.

I tugged on the manual inflate stem on the bottom of the raft and brought it to my mouth. When I first put the tube in my mouth, I tried to blow but couldn't create a seal around the tube. I reached up and touched my face for the first time. It felt like a dish of Playdough. My lips were deformed because of the windblast. The blood vessels in my face had burst under the slipstream pressure. Everything was utterly swollen and had no definition.

I stuck the tube back in my mouth and held it with my teeth while clamping my right hand around my lips. My lips were so puffed out; they fit into my first three fingers of my hand.

After blowing profusely for ten minutes, I inflated the bottom of the raft and then the spray shields. I had formed a floating pup tent—my own little cocoon. Then I began bailing out water from the raft with plastic bags from my survival kit. Finally, I began to warm up a little.

Feeling exhausted, I wanted to sleep but was afraid I'd never wake up again. Staring up into the sky, I could hear the other three F-15 crews searching for me. Up till now, I hadn't thought about Dennis. I was so worried about trying to save myself from drowning.

"Dennnnss . . . Dennnnss!" I cried out into the night. My bulging lips could barely form the syllables as I screamed at the top of my lungs for my backseater.

The crashing waves drowned out what little verbal syllables I could get out of my mouth. There was no reply.

Dozing in and out of consciousness, I tried to stay awake. I started thinking about my wife, Kristi, who was four months pregnant with our first child.

Four hours later, I spotted a light on the horizon. It moved back and forth across the waves. I knew it had to be a helicopter from its movements. I snatched the radio from my pack and turned it on to the emergency guard channel.

My fingers were frozen as I pressed the mic button, "Mayday! Mayday! Can anybody hear me?"

Nothing but static came over the speaker, so I tried again, "Can any—"

"Calling on guard, this is Coast Guard Rescue. Do you copy?" came over the radio.

I was elated when they replied.

"Roger, I copy," I replied. "This is Eagle 10 in the water; come twenty degrees right for three miles."

"Copy, right twenty for three miles," the voice replied.

"Rescue, don't get too close. I have two broken legs and one broken arm," I said, since the last thing I wanted was the rotor wash to knock me out of the raft.

"Roger, a man will jump out about twenty yards from your position with a litter and swim to you," they responded.

"Copy," I stated, feeling relieved.

The helicopter's lights and whooshing sound from the blades was upon me within a minute. I watched a man jump out of the helicopter as it hovered about fifteen feet above the water. I tried to move my limbs as he approached me, but they wouldn't respond.

"How ya doing?" the man said, approaching the raft.

"I'm frozen stiff and having difficulty moving," I said.

"You just stay where you are; I'll take care of you," he ordered.

After a few minutes, he had me secured in the litter. Waving to the helicopter, it maneuvered overhead and lowered a winch to connect to the litter. I felt like I was in a typhoon. The rotors kicked up the wind and waves, and it felt like needles were piercing my body. But worse yet, the rotors acted as a giant air conditioner, giving me another big chill.

"Are you ready?" the man asked.

I nodded my head.

As they started hauling me up, the basket spun wildly until they got me aboard.

"Don't worry, you're safe now," one of the pararescue guys yelled to me in the helicopter.

They lowered the winch again and picked up the man who helped me in the water. Then we flew to the nearest hospital, which happened to be in Wilmington, North Carolina.

Twenty or thirty doctors and nurses surrounded me when I arrived at the hospital. Underneath my flight suit, my T-shirt looked as though someone had taken a razor blade and shredded it. The laces on my boots were embedded into the leather. Within seconds I was buck naked, and they were taking X-rays of me. All I could think about was my good ole mom's advice, "Make sure you have clean underwear because you never know when you'll be in an accident."

I saw an orthopedic surgeon walk in through the maze of people. He went straight for my X-rays. I could hear him say, "Right knee is dislocated. Your left ankle is broken, and your left arm is dislocated."

I knew all this, I thought to myself. I could feel it.

"Can you give me some pain medication?" I asked him.

"Not yet," the surgeon replied. "We don't know the full extent of all your injuries."

Without a hi, hello, or how are you, the surgeon grabbed my right knee and "POP!" it back into place.

"Ahhhhhh," I screamed across the room.

Then he moved over to my left ankle, "POP!" Again I screamed as loud as I could. Then he repeated the same thing on my left arm.

Tears swelled in my eyes as I lay in agony without any pain medication. Finally, a nurse came along and gave me a shot of morphine. Within seconds, I slipped off into a happy place.

When I awoke, the Air Force informed me that my backseater, Dennis White, did not survive his ejection. It hurt losing a best friend, and took me a long time to recover.

Four surgeries later and six stainless steel screws in each leg, I was released to go home. I began an intensive physical therapy program to learn how to walk and possibly fly again. Two months later, I was able to take my first step.

I had to undergo several tests and get waivers to fly again. In February, ten months after my crash I was airborne again.

I soared over the same area where we crashed. My thoughts were on Dennis, but I knew he loved to fly too. It was hard; I loved flying and was excited to return to the cockpit. It's all I ever wanted to do.

If you crunch the numbers, I had about a half-second to spare. If I'd waited more than a half second, I would have impacted the water still in the seat.

CHAPTER 17

Lieutenant James M. Leavis
CH-53A Super Jolly

Lieutenant Leavis is the only marine pilot included in Pilots of Valor. I am sure plenty more Marine stories are out there, but finding them is difficult. When I first read this story, I was so impressed with his handling of the helicopter; I ranked it up there with the Medal of Honor stories.

* * *

I was excited as I drove to the base on a beautiful Southern California morning. Today, I was especially in high spirits because we were deploying to San Clemente Island with ten helicopters to support the Fifth Marines during their combat-readiness evaluation. It was the largest number of -53s I'd ever seen launched at one time.

Two months earlier, I had been designated a copilot in the CH-53A Super Jolly. I had flown a few special operations during the last month, and the sense of power I got from completing those simple tasks made me want more. On top of that, I was selected as the copilot to the mission commander, flying in the lead aircraft.

Pulling into Base Operations, I saw my aircraft commander. I liked the Major I was going to fly with. I was still very rank conscious since I was only a few months out of training in Pensacola. There Majors were treated with awe and reverence.

"Hey James, how are you doing?" the Major asked.

"Fine," I replied. "What time is the briefing?"

"We should be starting in about ten minutes," he replied.

Previously, I'd discovered the Major was friendly and showed genuine concern for us copilots and our training. He had recently transitioned from A-4s after three years out of the cockpit.

Ten minutes later, we kicked off our briefing. We divided the flight into sections and then we had individual flight crew briefings.

"Okay, does anybody have any questions about today's mission?" the Major asked everyone in attendance.

Everyone shook their heads their heads no. We'd been through this drill many times.

"All right, if we have an emergency, I'll come on the controls," the Major told me. "James, back me up in the checklist and come on the controls if I need help."

"Roger," I responded in agreement.

Pointing to me, the Major directed, "Call up the flight service station and see if they have any navigational outages for our flight route."

Heading over to the phone, I dialed the local flight service station and listened to the recording several times. There was nothing of importance that would affect our mission.

At the aircraft, I strapped in and ran through my preflight checklist. The fifteen-minute process was so ingrained in my consciousness; I could have done it with my eyes closed.

"I'm ready to start?" I stated.

"Roger, cranking," the Major replied, running through the start sequence.

I could hear the slow wind of the rotor, but the Nr tach generator gauge didn't register anything.

"Maj, we got a broken gauge," I stated.

"Crap," he replied. "Okay, shutting down. Chief, get maintenance over here to replace this gauge."

While the crew chief was calling maintenance, the Major called our wingman and told him we were going to be late and to take off without us. The ten-aircraft launch was broken into five sections, each staggered by fifteen minutes. We would jump in the middle after we got our gauge repaired.

Maintenance replaced the bad tach generator in minutes. I made my way through the start-up checklists again. This time the gauge worked correctly. The Major called for taxi, and we launched as a single aircraft.

Once we entered military airspace over Camp Pendleton, we checked in with range control to see if any of their ranges were hot. They weren't, so range control cleared us down the coast at 2,000 feet.

Keying the microphone, I said, "Pendleton Tower, this is Super Jolly One checking in near Pulgas Canyon."

"Roger, Jolly One, radar contact," the controller replied.

Since takeoff, I had been doing my copilot duties, striving for precision and looking to the Major for approval. He finally gave me the controls of the helicopter.

"I'm going to descend from 2,000 to 1,000 feet," I said, feeling confident.

"Sounds good to me," he replied calmly.

I lowered the collective slightly to begin the gradual letdown to 1,000 feet, our proper altitude for the MACS 7 checkpoint and entry into Camp Pendleton's pattern.

Suddenly, a loud "*Clunk!*" came from behind my seat.

At first, I thought I had done something wrong. Then, immediately the helicopter rolled left wing down twenty degrees, and the nose dropped fifteen degrees below the horizon. I was looking straight at the ground.

A yaw to the right quickly developed, which I countered with some left rudder and then complete left rudder with aft right cyclic. At this point, my day turned into a nightmare, and my life changed forever.

"Tail-rotor drive failure!" I screamed in a strained voice.

The Major responded calmly and said, "I have the helicopter," as he took the controls from me.

"We need to autorotate," I yelled.

"Relax and secure the yaw servo," he replied calmly.

Not understanding what he meant, I quickly turned to the Major and said, "What?"

He made no reply.

As I glanced out my window, the roll was becoming more severe at nearly 45 degrees, and the aircraft was now 20 degrees nose down and yawing severely to the right. I was terrified. Fully aware that our lives were in danger, I continued my copilot duties.

Bracing against my side window, I pulled myself up in the seat by grabbing the right side of my seat to reach the center console. The Major wasn't doing anything.

"Maj, we need to autorotate," I screamed again.

No response.

Ten seconds had elapsed since I'd relinquished the controls. First, I punched off the AMP and then the yaw servo. Almost simultaneously with the securing of the yaw servo button, the aircraft started rolling to the left, becoming completely ballistic.

The helicopter was rolling rapidly along its central axis while spinning around its center of gravity. I was thrown against my window again, cutting my head as the helicopter tumbled wildly. Out of the corner of my eye, I saw the crew chief and the first mechanic trying to brace themselves near the open crew door. They couldn't hold on, and both spilled out the door. Oh my God, I thought, we've lost everybody in the back.

The Major's hands were glued on the controls, and his eyes gleamed straight ahead. I turned back to my instruments. I checked the collective and noted that it was full down. That wasn't right. It should be back, I told myself. All the caution lights were flashing after each roll, but other than that, the gauges appeared normal.

My gyro in my head was spinning freely following the aircraft's erratic motions.

Reaching over, I lowered the landing gear and said in a frantic voice over the radio, "Mayday! Mayday! We're going down."

"This is Camp Pen—"

Screaming over the radio, I yelled, "I'm going to secure the engines."

Again, the Major didn't respond.

I assumed he concurred with my decision since he made no response and I took control of the engines. Adrenaline was pumping wildly through my body. I was lucid, but I couldn't fathom why this happened. I understood the initial indications and passed them on to the Major. It was obviously a drive-shaft failure, but why were we rolling? At this time, I knew I was going to die as I watched the ground rushing up.

A disjointed thought raced through my mind: I hoped that dying wouldn't hurt too much and prayed that it wouldn't be by fire. I used all my strength to put my right hand on the speed-control levers. The lateral Gs were enormous, and the simple act of lifting my arm was tough.

My hand found the speed-control levers in between the Major and me. Slamming them back, I tried to shut them down, but they wouldn't move aft because there was a foot was in the way. At first, I was utterly puzzled. Why was there a foot in the way when nobody else was in the helicopter but the Major and myself? Seconds later, I realized the crew chief and first mechanic had secured themselves with the gunners' belts. Apparently, they had climbed back into the aircraft after a few terrifying seconds suspended in space with the crew chief's foot lodged in the speed-control unit.

Forgetting about the levers, I turned my attention to the front panel. The rolling stopped suddenly after six complete turns, but the aircraft spun at a sickening rate.

"Airspeed 50, altimeter 600 feet and descending," I hollered.

Passing below the ridgeline, I kept my reference on a lone scrub oak adorning the otherwise barren crest. The Nr increased to 125 percent, and I contemplated raising the collective a bit to bring it down.

Glancing over at the Major, he was still holding onto the controls but not moving them. I decided to keep the collective the same since the rolling stopped. Also, I feared that if I decreased the Nr, the rolling might start again.

I could see every detail on the ground becoming more prominent as we dropped out of the sky. The radar altimeter was giving me pretty stable readings. As we had briefed, I read out every hundred feet below the 500-foot mark. I expected the Major to flare the helicopter at each interval, but he didn't.

I started thinking I was the only man left alive in the helicopter. I'd seen the crew lying helplessly in the back, and the Major hadn't said a word to me since he told me to turn off the servos. His hands were still on the controls, but why wasn't he talking to me? At least he could acknowledge me, I thought.

"Autorotate! Autorotate!" I screamed again.

Why wasn't he complying with the book? We should have autorotated immediately. The last thing he told me was to shut off the yaw servos. Why had he done that? That had nothing to do with our emergency.

I was still absolutely terrified. I began to suspect the Major was dead. I watched as we plowed through the altitude at which we should have started our flair. Instinctively, I moved my left hand to the collective.

My right hand was still on the speed-control levers, so I wrapped my knees around the cyclic to keep it somewhat steady. When the radar altimeter read fifty feet, I pulled the collective back as hard as possible. The hell with the Major, I thought. I wasn't going to die.

The helicopter hit the ground hard but flat. It made a quarter turn to the right before coming to a complete stop.

Debris hit me from all sides and forced me to turn my head to the right in time to witness the Major's seat explode from its moorings and exit through the overhead green-house window. I remember being awed by the sight, thinking it looked like an ejection, even though we did not have ejection seats.

Everything went in slow motion as I saw the rotor blades strike the ground at the one o'clock position, break up, and fly toward the right side of the cockpit.

Shrapnel hit my helmet, and I felt pain in my right ear. I looked down at my right hand, wondering why it no longer responded to my demands. Staring at my arm, I could tell the impact shattered my arm above the wrist, but there was no pain. My situation was difficult, but I was alive and somewhat intact.

"Get out! Get out!" I screamed as loud as I could in hopes someone might hear me.

While unstrapping, I turned right to exit by the crew door. Suddenly a fireball leaped forward, forcing me back into my seat. Something in the rear had exploded. Sitting back in my chair, I covered my mouth and nose with my hand as smoke and flames whirled inside. Waiting for the fire to dissipate, I jumped out the Major's window.

After leaving the aircraft, I ran some distance away and threw my helmet and kneeboard down. Returning to the wreck, I fought through the smoke and flames and found the crew chief and first mechanic. I dragged them both thirty yards away from the fireball, I still couldn't feel any pain from my broken arm. One of the men was dead, and the other was bleeding profusely from his nose and mouth. I put them down gently and headed back to the helicopter to search for the Major.

Dazed, I fell face-first into the dirt. Minutes passed, and I couldn't remember how long I had stayed there.

"Lieutenant, are you all right?" someone said in a soft female voice.

Groggy, I responded, "What?"

"I'm a nurse," she said. "Are you okay?"

"Yeah, I think so."

Rolling over, I could see her white uniform. The mental barrier I had erected was returning. I could feel the burns on the back of my neck and head from the seat belts.

"What happened?" I asked, standing up.

"Your helicopter crashed," she replied.

I started to get up and head back to the wreckage and said, "I have to help the others."

She yelled at me, "Let them go, lieutenant; you can't help them. They're gone."

I was in shock, and it took me a few seconds to register what she was saying.

She chased me from behind, grabbed me by the collar, and said, "You're in shock, and you need to lie down."

"I have to get—"

"No!" she ordered.

I followed her instructions, and suddenly, I became exhausted. I woke up to find myself strapped into a stretcher and carried to a waiting ambulance for the short trip to Camp Pendleton Hospital.

I found out later the nurse at the scene of our crash was taking her husband (a gunnery sergeant) to work at Los Pulgas. Our ballistic helicopter almost swatted their truck from the road as it passed directly over them. She was at my side within minutes.

I have relived each horrifying second of that flight a thousand times over. My inactions were partially responsible for the deaths of three outstanding aircrew members. If I had entered the autorotation immediately after recognizing the drive-shaft failure, the aircraft would have remained somewhat controllable. Instead, I'd relied on the Major to handle the emergency. He was the first to die. He suffered an aneurysm (a ruptured artery in the brain) almost immediately after the onset of the aircraft rolls. I had indeed been on my own.

CHAPTER 18

Anonymous

KC-135 Stratotanker

Sometimes malfunctions are not the fault of mankind. Sometimes, Mother Nature can deal an aircrew with a lousy hand. The crew of this KC-135 performed admirably in a horrific moment. With their aircraft burning and only seconds to escape, their training saved their lives. They are Pilots of Valor.

* * *

I was getting tired. Rubbing my eyes, I checked my watch. Three-thirty in the morning it read. It had been a long day, and I was ready to call it quits. Our mission had been relatively routine, with two air refuelings and a navigation leg behind us. Finally, we were on the last part of our flight, two instrument approaches.

The sky was cloudless as I strained to spot the runway on final approach. I was in the left seat, supervising a student pilot's approaches and landings. The upgrade pilot was in the jump seat monitoring the approaches. A student navigator, along with an instructor navigator, was just behind him. Two boom operators were also strapped in the back of the plane.

I watched the copilot in the right seat land the aircraft 1,500 feet down the runway. He landed on the right side, just missing the centerline. He was a little nervous as I graded his landings. After placing the throttles to idle, he corrected back to the center of the runway.

"Flaps and trim," he said softly.

"Roger," I replied as I brought the flaps back up. I was resetting the trim back to the takeoff setting when I noticed something outside my window. An object on the fringe of the landing lights caught my eye. I thought maybe it was the discoloration of the runway.

"Throttles coming up," said the copilot, shoving the levers forward.

There it was again. A flock of birds, I thought.

Focusing, it hit me! It wasn't discoloration or birds. "Watch out!" I screamed. "Cows straight ahead."

"Oh my God," was all the copilot could spit out.

I realized what was going to happen to us, and two seconds later, it did!

0 Seconds—After Impact.

I watched in horror as the cows went underneath our fuselage. Cringing, I heard, "*Chunk. . . . Thunk.*"

The copilot reacted immediately, "Tower, we've just hit some cows; activate the crash rescue!"

Instantaneously, I glanced down to check our speed. The airspeed indicator read 130 knots.

2 Seconds

"Hey, what's going on up there?" one of the boom operators broke in over the intercom without hearing our previous radio calls. "Did we blow some tires?" he said, getting out of his seat.

3 Seconds

My hands instinctively came on the controls as the nose of the aircraft settled to the runway.

Screaming, I said, "Our nose gear just collapsed."

The screeching sound of the nose gear echoed throughout the cabin as it was violently forced back against the belly of the aircraft, rupturing the forward body fuel tank. Ten thousand pounds of JP-4 fuel began spilling on the runway. Immediately it ignited.

"Fire!" someone from the back cried out.

I threw my right hand forward to the throttles, as they were still in takeoff power, and yanked them back to idle.

"Brace yourself! We're going to crash," I screamed.

5 Seconds

Everything became chaotic. I felt the left wing lower as I tried to counteract with the right aileron. I glanced out the left side and saw sparks as the wingtip scraped against the concrete. The plane started to veer left, off the runway. I threw in full right rudder.

"Co, help me with the rudder!" I ordered.

"Full right rudder," he replied, as he stomped on the rudder.

The airplane slowly started to respond as the rudder took effect and kept us going straight. Out of the corner of my right eye, I could see the people behind me watching helplessly. Mouths wide open as the copilot and I tried to control the airplane. The full right rudder kept the aircraft on the runway at 125 knots.

The boom operator in the back yelled, "We have a fire moving across our left wing."

Swiveling my head, I could see the glow from a giant orange and red fireball coming from that wing. We were in some serious trouble, I told myself. The fire wouldn't take long to ignite the rest of our fuel and engulf the entire plane.

6 Seconds

"We have fire from the right wing too," the other boom operator chimed in.

I hollered, "Brakes." We both slammed our feet to the floor with little effect. We were traveling too fast.

"Oh no!" someone yelled on the intercom. "We have a fire inside the aircraft in the rear cargo bay."

"Everyone in the back, come forward," I screamed.

My copilot's eyes said it all. I'm sure he could see the same from mine. Pure fear! Nothing in the world could have prepared us for this. We weren't going to make it, I thought. We already had a fire inside the airplane and were still screaming down the runway.

"Nav, get the escape ropes," I yelled.

"Roger," he replied, unhooking the emergency escape ropes from the cockpit ceiling.

7 Seconds

Another look out the left window, and I could see both engine pods scraping on the runway.

"Airspeed, 100 knots," said the copilot.

I could feel the rudder becoming mushy as the airplane slowed. I started to apply more pressure to the right brake as I took my foot off the left one. The effect was minimal but enough to keep the aircraft on the runway, at least for a couple more seconds.

"Here's the escape ropes," the instructor navigator said, draping one rope over the hook above the crew entry chute. "I have another rope for you," he said, throwing the rope over my shoulder.

8 Seconds

"Oh God, the flames are coming closer," said the student Nav.

"Is everybody up front," I inquired.

"Yes," the instructor navigator replied.

9 Seconds

"We're all here," a boom operator hollered, bracing himself against the navigator consul. "The fire in the cargo compartment is getting closer. We'll have to escape through the cockpit windows."

"Close the crew door," I replied.

Then the copilot asked, "Can we use the crew entry chute?"

"Negative! The door is wedged against the concrete," came the reply from somebody.

"All right, everybody, we go out the pilots' windows," I said as the aircraft began sliding out of control on the runway.

10 Seconds

The aircraft was slowing, but all my attempts to keep it straight failed. The plane quickly snapped to the left. I could only watch as we departed between the 3,000 and 2,000 remaining markers.

"Brace yourself," I hollered again.

Bouncing into the infield, the copilot yelled, "Watch out."

Everyone was forward, and those unable to strap in braced themselves the best way they could. We waited and watched as the aircraft swerved hard to the left, and rapidly decelerated. The next five seconds were the most terrifying in my life. I couldn't do anything but ride along. I couldn't start egressing until the plane came to a stop. I felt completely helpless. Finally, the giant aircraft came to a halt.

15 Seconds

The airplane slid 180 degrees to the left and came to a rest facing downwind 230 feet from the edge of the runway.

"Go! Go! Go!" I screamed, trying to cut the throttles off.

My adrenaline was so great I squeezed the throttles together too tightly, and they wouldn't move. I saw the upgrade pilot reach forward over the throttle quadrant and pull the fire switches. With one hand, the copilot opened his window and started to crawl out.

The entire area around our aircraft lit up like a night baseball game as more fuel caught fire. In a few more seconds, it would all explode.

17 Seconds

The copilot was out his window in a split second. Standing on the top of the window ledge, the upgrade pilot threw a rope between his ankles.

I watched the copilot jump six feet straight to the ground without the rope. He was running as fast as he could away from the plane.

19 Seconds

I opened my window and threw my rope out. The heat was extremely intense as it poured inside the cockpit. The fire was blazing out of control now. I struggled out my window, sliding down the rope and hitting the dirt headfirst. My survival instincts took over now as I jumped up and ran away from the burning inferno. I could see my copilot a hundred feet ahead of me, still running as I stopped.

20 Seconds

Turning around, I saw the upgrade pilot climbing out the copilot's window. Using the handholds above the window, he quickly lowered himself using the Pitot tube as a step on the way down.

23 Seconds

The boom operator popped his head through my window. He went head first, diving out the window. On the way to the ground, I saw him grab the hot Pitot tube to break his fall. Fortunately for him, he had his gloves on since the tube was blistering hot.

24 Seconds

Next, the student navigator came out of the copilot's window. Holding the rope upside down, he lowered himself slowly until his legs came out of the window. He turned right side up in one quick motion while holding on to the rope for dear life.

As the student navigator hit the ground, I yelled, "Over here." Hearing me, he steadied his legs, then ran toward me.

27 Seconds

The instructor navigator was next. Barely holding onto the rope, he fell six feet to the ground, hitting hard.

Turning around, I started counting. "One. . . . Two. . . . Three. . . . Four. . . . Five. . . . Six," I was missing one.

"Where's the other boom operator?" I screamed.

No one answered. I looked for a head in either escape window, but there was nothing. The Instructor navigator got up and started running for us when I saw the other boom operator's head poke out of the copilot's window.

30 Seconds

The boom operator hung halfway out the copilot's window. I moved closer to help out, but a gust of wind blew scorching air over me. The heat hit me like an oven as I raised my arm to shield my eyes.

The boom operator was also engulfed in the heat as he dropped to the ground, lying on his stomach and hugging the dirt. The heat was so intense I didn't think the boom operator would make it.

Lying flat on his stomach, the boom operator didn't move.

35 Seconds

I saw my instructor navigator running back to the airplane to help the boom operator. By now, the burning lake of fuel was moving very close to us. The heat made it hard to see and breathe.

40 Seconds

"Kaboooom."

The explosion jolted me forward. I could tell the plane was losing its will to live.

"Get down!" I screamed over the explosion. Flaming metal parts of debris launched into the air, falling all around us. I could see the instructor navigator and the last boom operator running past me to safety. Thank God, I thought.

45 Seconds

We assembled well clear of the wreckage.

"Boom . . . Boom . . . Kaboom. . . . Kaboom."

More explosions ripped our airplane apart. The entire aircraft was engulfed in flames.

I ran to the arriving fire trucks with all of us accounted for and informed them that everyone was safe.

The most amazing aspect of our whole ordeal was that no one panicked. All the crewmembers, for the most part, stayed calm. Those few moments skidding down the runway were just enough time to plan our escapes. If anyone of us had caused a delay in egressing from the airplane, someone would have died.

PRISONER OF WAR

"One of the greatest sacrifices for one's country."

I close out Pilots of Valor with two Prisoner of War stories. Even though these two individuals did not receive valor in the cockpit, they carried valor into captivity. Their stories are truly heart-wrenching.

Nearing the magic 100-mission number that would end his combat tour, the airman prayed that he could continue to dodge the flak and the deadly Surface to Air Missiles. He knew that a massive rescue effort would be triggered if he were shot down. He also realized that those unlucky enough to be captured would join a group of men dedicated to resisting their captors.

Most of the prisoners in Vietnam were Air Force, and Navy pilots and navigators shot down over the North. The typical Air Force prisoner was a fighter pilot who had survived a bailout from a crippled F-105, F-4, or F-100. Sometimes he could evade his pursuers for days, but often his parachute was spotted, and he was captured immediately.

The airman knew that the war did not end if he was captured. Bound by the long-standing tradition of the American fighting man and the Code of Conduct, he would be obligated to resist and oppose the enemy while in captivity.

President Eisenhower in 1955 prescribed the 247-word Code of Conduct. Under the Code, POWs are required to make every effort to escape and aid others to escape. The senior-ranking prisoner must take command, and all subordinates will obey his lawful orders. Though giving name, rank, service number, and date of birth is mandatory, American service members will evade answering further questions to the utmost of their ability.

Failing to abide by the Geneva Convention, the communists resorted to torture and brainwashing, forcing the Americans to reveal military information or denounce their government. A prisoner, tortured to the breaking point, who responded to the interrogator's questions, knew he was fully responsible for his statements. Military authorities would examine the man's conduct and the circumstances of his captivity upon repatriation.

Though unsuccessful, the attempts in 1970 to rescue the POWs in the daring Son Tay prison raid demonstrated to the world that America had not forgotten her bravest sons.

In February 1973, the first POWs were released by the North Vietnamese. By the end of March, all surviving prisoners had been repatriated. Navy Lieutenant Commander Everett Alvarez, Jr., a captive for eight and one-half years, was the longest-held pilot. Sixteen Air Force men reportedly died in captivity, and 324 returned.

In 1973, after almost six years of captivity, Lieutenant Colonel Leo Thorsness was awarded the Medal of Honor for his heroic 1967 mission. Leo described his reaction as, "I was proud and humble, but prison taught me there are other things that test a man more than combat. At no time in the airplane did I ever fear? There's a certain security in the cockpit. In prison, you are by yourself, and it continues daily. Unfortunately, Medals of Honor are not presented under the most trying test of a man's courage, bravery, and capabilities." Leo's statement proved prophetic.

CHAPTER 19

Captain Lance Peter Sijan
F-4C Phantom
Medal of Honor

When I first read this story, I almost cried. The story of Lance P. Sijan is one of the most incredible prisoners of war stories ever told. After reading this story, you will agree Lance is a true American hero in every sense of the word.

* * *

My R&R in Bangkok needed to be longer. Sitting in the back seat of my F-4, I reflected on the tape I had made for my family in Thailand. I especially missed my little sister Janine.

"Lance, you ready to go?" my front seater John asked.

Breaking my trance, I said, "Roger, I'm as ready as I'll ever be."

"Okay, let's start engines," John said.

I could hear Colonel John W. Armstrong, commander of the 366th Tactical Fighter Squadron, talking to the crew chief as both engines rotated to life. Today was my first mission after my R&R, and I struggled to concentrate on all the checklist items.

Fifteen minutes later, we were airborne. Our mission today was a target in North Vietnam near the Laos border.

After disconnecting from the tanker, we sped deeper into enemy territory.

"Scopes clean," I said. Everything seemed too calm in the North as not even a MiG was out and about.

"Two miles to target," Colonel Armstrong replied. "I'm starting my run now."

Colonel Armstrong lined up on our target by lowering the nose and shoving the throttles to full power.

Suddenly, out of nowhere, flashes of light appeared off of our right wing.

Screaming toward the target, the tracers from antiaircraft guns were closing in on our position. "Guns on the right," I called.

Instantly, Colonel Armstrong rolled the aircraft, trying to avoid the incoming bullets. It was useless as one found our fuel tank and blew off our right wing, sending us out of control.

"Bailout!" was all I heard as I reached for my ejection handle. After seeing our wing depart from the aircraft, the decision to eject was already made for me. The force of the ejection was incredible. As I headed up the rails, my whole face stretched like a rubber band. The instantaneous Gs slapped my body deep inside the ejection seat as I rocketed skyward.

The first thing I saw when my eyes opened was our F-4 disintegrating in mid-air. I would have been vaporized in the fireball if I had stayed with the aircraft another second.

I only had a quick moment to check my canopy before unknowingly hitting the ground. My feet slipped out in front while my head flew backward, impacting the dirt. Excruciating pain ran throughout my body. The force of the impact on my skull left me dazed and confused while I lay on the ground. It felt like an eternity before I could sit up and re-cage my gyros.

My head was pounding, and blood dripped down my neck. I almost died when I saw my right hand. Three of my fingers were bent back toward my wrist. Checking my left leg, I saw a bone protruding through my flight suit as blood spilled onto the ground. I knew I was in real trouble, and I was alone.

Glancing upward, I could hear aircraft circling overhead. Darting back and forth, trying to locate Colonel Armstrong and me. Virtually immobilized, I started to propel myself backward using my elbows and buttocks to make it to a clearing in the trees.

Resting at the edge, I took my radio out of my side pocket and turned it on. Immediately I could hear chattering from the rescue.

"AWOL 1, can you hear me?" came of the radio.

Momentarily forgetting about my injuries and concentrating on my rescue, I said, "This is AWOL 1; I hear you loud and clear."

"AWOL 1, please authenticate," the voice immediately responded. "Who's the greatest football team in the world?"

Most Wisconsins didn't need to think about that question and neither did I.

"The Green Bay Packers," I replied.

"Authentication correct. AWOL 1, do you know the condition of your front-seater?" the replied.

"Negative," talking louder and faster I said, "I didn't see him get out of the aircraft."

Ground fire erupted from all directions as a large Jolly Green helicopter sprang over the hill. I positioned myself so the HH-3E could see me through the brush.

"AWOL 1, Jolly 15 has you in sight; stay where you are; let us come to you."

The Jolly Green helicopter hovered nearby for thirty minutes as rifle shots kept him from coming closer. The bullets made a distinct "*ping*" sound as they impacted the green chopper. Then the lone rifle was replaced by multiple gunshots echoing throughout the jungle.

I watched patiently as the helicopter came under a withering hail of fire. Then, without warning, the helicopter left the area. My heart sank to the bottom of my stomach as I watched them go over the hill.

Soon the sun dropped below the horizon. Hearing voices throughout the jungle, I crawled under some bushes and hid along with all my gear. I focused on preparing myself for a pick-up in the morning. Wrapping my leg with strips of my parachute, I made a small tourniquet to keep the bone from protruding anymore. The dark red blood soon discolored the shiny material, but at least the bleeding had stopped. Later that night, the pain began to set in. Sleep was impossible, as I wanted dearly to scream out loud into the night sky.

In the morning, I could see friendly aircraft flying overhead. Keying up my radio, I said, "This is AWOL 1. Does anybody read me?"

Nobody answered. After several unanswered calls, I concluded my radio was broken. I needed a signaling device. I searched for my emergency survival kit, which contained a mirror and several flares, but I couldn't find it. I must have lost it during the ejection, I thought to myself.

Why didn't they come back for me? Did they not see me yesterday? I retraced all my training to remember if I was doing something wrong. I couldn't think of anything.

As night set again, I started planning to move out in the morning. I knew the North Vietnamese were near and would find me before too long. I had a good idea that I was near Vihn, and the only way to freedom was to the East. I made up my mind to start crawling as soon as daylight broke.

Early on the third day, I headed out. Moving at a snail's pace, I crawled for about an hour and then rested for a bit. It took every ounce of energy I had to move a few feet. Once rested, I continued across the jungle floor.

Days passed into nights as I moved only yards at a time. I was growing weaker every day without food and water. I began licking the water from the leaves and chewing on pieces of vegetation. Some days, I couldn't move at all. I was too exhausted.

After four weeks of crawling through the jungle, I became so weak that my ribs started to protrude through my chest. Every muscle and bone in my body hurt. I knew I had to find help, or else I wouldn't survive.

Two weeks later, I found a dirt road and stopped. I couldn't go on further. I crawled onto the road and lay there, waiting for friendly forces to come along. The next day a truck of North Vietnamese regular troops saw me through the jungle.

Jubilant at capturing an American flyer, they kicked and poked me while screaming at me in Vietnamese. Eventually, they loaded me in the truck and hauled me to a holding camp. It was around Christmas day. My six weeks of trying to evade the enemy ended, at least for the time being, I told myself.

They took me to a small hut and threw me on a straw mat on the floor. Pain raced through my spine. The flesh around my buttocks was worn down to my hip bones. It was one giant raw scab.

A little while later, a man brought me some food. It was the first solid food I had since I ejected.

The following day, I felt a lot better. Some of my strength returned. Then my Serbian ancestral fighting instincts took over. Lying on the mat, I waited until only one guard was in the room.

"Hey, can you help me?" I whispered.

Barely hearing me, the guard got up from his seat and walked closer. When he bent over to see what I wanted, I swung my left hand and karate-chopped him across his face. Immediately he hit the dirt out cold. It hurt like hell, but it also felt good.

With the guard unconscious, I crawled through a small hole in the hut and headed for the jungle. My emotions were high as I felt freedom again. I made my way deeper and deeper into the jungle. I could hear them hunting for me as I crawled quickly as possible. Finally, they were upon me. Hiding behind some leaves, I froze in place.

One of the guards followed my boot marks along the jungle floor and walked right up to me. My freedom had only lasted for two hours.

They transported me to a prison camp on the night of New Year's. My strength was slowly evaporating when we arrived. A short, mean-looking interrogator called the Rodent was the first person to enter my cell. Immediately the beatings began.

"I want to know about your strike plans?" the Rodent asked.

Sizing the man up, I knew he would probably stop at nothing to get what he wanted, but I was prepared for him.

"I don't know what you're talking about," I answered back.

"Your arm, your arm, it is very bad. I will twist it unless you tell me," he said, moving closer.

"Go to hell! I'm not going to tell you," I yelled at him.

Suddenly, the Rodent jumped on me and started twisting my mangled arm.

"Ahhhhhh!"

"Tell me, or I'll keep hurting you," he demanded.

"Kiss my—"

"Ahhhhhhh!" I screamed. "You son-of-a-bitch. Wait till I get my strength back."

"Name?. What is your name?" he shouted in my face.

"My name is Sijan!" I told him in a broken voice. "My name is Lance Peter Sijan, you bastard."

Then he started kicking my broken leg. The pain was unbearable as I lay on the cold concrete floor. The interrogation went on for an hour and a half. Over and over again, the Rodent kept beating me. Then it ended as suddenly as it started. I felt in good spirits; I knew I had won the first round without giving up any information.

The following day, they stuck me in a bamboo cell. At first, I tried to dig my way out. Then one of the guards saw me and bashed me on the head with a stick. Blood trickled from my wounds as he continued hitting me. Finally, he quit from exhaustion.

Later I untied some of the cords holding the side poles together and almost escaped before they caught me. Again, they made me pay dearly for trying to escape.

After several days, the North Vietnamese prepared us so they could transport all the prisoners to Hanoi. With my energy almost entirely gone, I could only lie on the dirt floor of my cell and wait for someone to help me.

Two American prisoners walked toward me. "Come on buddy, let us help you get into the truck," one of them said.

In a weak voice, I replied, "Thank you."

"My name is Robert Craner," the man replied.

Glancing at the other man, I said, "I know you, your Guy Gruters, aren't you?" as I struggled to get each word out.

The man picked me up and responded, "Yea, how did you know?"

"We were at the academy together," I replied. "Don't you know me? I'm Lance Sijan."

At first, the man was puzzled, but then he became white as a ghost and said, "My God, Lance, is that you?"

I nodded.

"We played football together, didn't we?" Guy asked.

"Yea," I said, feeling better. "How the hell are we going to get out of here? Do you think we can steal one of their guns? I made it once; I can do it again."

Guy looked straight into my eyes as he laid me on the truck. "Lance, don't worry about escaping yet," he responded.

"I'm ready whenever you guys are," I said, smiling at him.

Then the Rodent came over to the truck. Turning to Bob and Guy, he said, "Sijan is a very difficult man. He struck a guard and injured him. He ran away from us. You must not let him do that anymore."

Then the truck started to move, and my world went blank. The grueling truck ride to Hanoi took several days. At one stop, they stuffed us under a canvas cover.

"Lance," Craner said, shaking me.

I struggled to open my eyes. "Yea," I replied.

"You have to stay awake and eat something," he directed, as he fed me spoonfuls of rice.

It hurt to eat. Life was draining from my body. I was too weak even to stay awake.

"Lance, tell me about your ejection?" Craner asked.

I took a couple of deep breaths and said, "Our plane was hit, and I broke my fingers and leg."

Pausing, "I had to crawl to get to freedom. I evaded for forty-five days." Then I fell asleep again.

During the night, we took off again. We were getting closer to Hanoi every day. The truck constantly bounced up and down in the back along the bumpy roads.

Then Bob said, "He's dead, Guy."

Opening my eyes, I replied in a raspy voice, "I'm not dead yet," I said, looking straight into Guy's eyes as he massaged my face and neck.

"I'm going to escape," I said proudly.

Bob responded, "My hat's off to you, ole buddy."

Then everything went black again.

Finally, we reached Hanoi. They put the three of us into a cell called "Little Vegas." It was dark, with open air, and a pool of water on the worn cement floor. We were all chilled to the bone. I was always shivering and shaking uncontrollably.

"Lance, can I get anything for you?" Craner asked.

"No, I'm fine. Just give me a few days, and I'll be ready to escape," I replied.

Then a Vietnamese medic came into our cell and gave me a shot of yellow fluid. I had no idea what it was. For some reason, it didn't matter. He did nothing for my open sores and wounds. Picking up my mangled hand, he shook his head and walked away.

At night a guard opened the little window on our door and looked in.

"Come here," I said, raising my hand to karate chop him. I wondered if I could get him inside, but he closed the window and turned away. I wanted to nail him right in the kisser.

When the sun rose, I asked Bob and Guy to help me exercise to build up my strength for another escape attempt. They propped me up on my cot and waved my arms around a few times. It took all the energy I could muster to do that simple task.

"Hey Robert, how about going out and getting me a burger and fries?" I asked.

He chuckled at me and said, "Sure thing, Lance."

Coughing and having trouble breathing, I became exhausted and fell back asleep.

The next day, Guy woke me up and asked how I was doing. I tried to speak, but the words would not come out.

"Lance, just blink your eyes once if you're okay?" I blinked once and then dozed off.

We had been in Hanoi for eight days. My strength was sapped, and I could feel myself slowly slipping. At night, my voice returned, and I began yelling, "Dad, Dad, where are you? Come here; I need you!"

On 21 January, the guards came in and got me. The last thing I remember was the happy times I spent with my family and my little sister Janine, and then I closed my eyes for the last time.

Lance P. Sijan was born on 13 April 1942 in Milwaukee, Wisconsin. He graduated from the Air Force Academy and was commissioned in June 1965. After pilot training at Laredo, Texas, Captain Sijan was assigned to jet fighter duty at George Air Force Base, California.

In July 1967, he was assigned to Danang Air Base, Republic of Vietnam. In November, his F-4C Phantom was shot down over North Vietnam. Captain Sijan was declared missing in action until his death in captivity was confirmed.

In addition to the Medal of Honor, he won the Distinguished Flying Cross, the Air Medal with five oak leaf clusters, and the Purple Heart with one cluster.

Today, one of the highest awards the Air Force gives its members is the Lance P. Sijan Award.

CHAPTER 20

Lt. Commander John S. McCain III
A-4 Skyhawk

Senator John McCain's story is another incredible American Prisoner of War story. Imagine bailing out of your jet in a lake with two broken arms and a broken leg. We conclude Pilots of Valor with an American Hero, excelling as a US military pilot.

* * *

I grabbed my flight gear and left the *USS Oriskany's* briefing room.

"You'd better be careful," Strike Operations Officer Lew Chatham told me. "We're probably going to lose someone on this mission."

Smiling, I replied, "You don't have to worry about me, Lew."

I was charged up and feeling confident on my twenty-third combat sortie. The day before, I had taken out three North Vietnamese MiG fighters sitting on an apron at Phuc Yen airfield. I was ready for some more action.

Strapped into the cockpit, I enjoyed the beautiful October morning as I waited my turn to take off. As a part of a twenty-ship formation, we were scheduled to take out a power plant on the western edge of Hanoi. The mission was going to be dicey at best.

The catapult ride was a burst of exhilaration as I went airborne off the carrier. Sucking up the gear, I checked in on the radio, "Raider 21's up."

"Copy, rejoin right side," my flight lead responded.

Closing in tighter, I planted my Skyraider into formation with the other aircraft. After all twenty ships were aloft, we proceeded on our way.

Before long, we were approaching land. The rattlesnake buzzing sound in my headset started as soon as we went feet dry. Vietnamese radars were active and trying to lock onto us.

"Raider 21, go extended and follow me," lead directed.

"Roger," I replied.

Closing in on the target, I set myself up a quarter mile behind my flight lead. Suddenly, surface-to-air missiles started flying everywhere. My instrument panel lit up, telling me a SAM had locked onto my aircraft as I put the power plant in the cross hairs.

"Raider 21, missile in the air," someone in my flight yelled.

I immediately punched off some chaff, trying to confuse the missile's guidance system, it worked. I then reverted my attention to the power plant and pickled off my bombs.

Slamming the stick backward, I began pulling out of the dive as hard as possible. Russian-built missiles were leaving streaks all over the sky. Without warning, one exploded to my right. Swiveling my head, I saw my right wing had been sheared off. It was a horrifying sight.

Instantly, my plane began spiraling inverted toward the ground. I was completely out of control.

"Mayday! Mayday!" I screamed. "Raider 21 is going in."

Rocketing toward the ground at five hundred knots, I reached up with both hands and pulled the ejection handle. Immediately, the Skyhawk's canopy blew off, and the ejection seat launched me upward. The internal forces on my body were so great I passed out for a few seconds.

I regained consciousness just before I hit the water as I checked for my helmet and oxygen mask. Both were gone and ripped off my face by the force of the ejection. Suddenly the water was upon me before I could inflate my life preserve. The lake was in the middle of downtown Hanoi was not where I wanted to be.

I sank twenty feet to the bottom without floatation. I couldn't locate the toggle for my life preserver to inflate it. I kicked off the bottom, trying to propel myself to the top. In a semi-state of shock, I felt no pain.

Finally, I made it to the surface. Gulping in a deep breath, I started sinking again. My fifty-pound survival equipment was pulling me under water. As I went down a second time, I tried to find the toggle to inflate it, but my arms weren't moving for me.

I pushed up from the bottom a second time but with less force. I almost made it to the top but started going back under again. I couldn't understand why moving my arms and legs was so hard. Dizzy and holding my breath, I finally got my life vest toggle in my mouth and yanked it with my teeth. Instantly the vest inflated and lifted me to the surface.

Fighting for all the air I could breathe, I threw my head back and floated there, trying to get my senses aligned.

Two soldiers swam out a minute or two later and pulled me to shore. Hundreds of people were gathered around to watch. They began yelling and cursing at me as one lady came up and spat in my face. I didn't let it bother me. Puzzled, I couldn't figure out why all the people were out in the open while we were bombing their city.

Lying on the ground, one of the two men that pulled me out of the lake started screaming at me. After a few seconds, I realized he wanted me to remove my clothes, but I couldn't move my arms.

I raised my head and was stunned to see that my right leg was nearly perpendicular to my knee. My leg was severely crushed at the knee joint.

"My God, my leg!" I screamed.

Enraged and uptight, the crowd began yelling even louder. I don't know what set them off, but it didn't matter; I couldn't understand a word they were saying.

Looking at my arms, I could tell both were broken, especially my right one in multiple places.

Suddenly the guy started yanking my clothes off for me.

"Ahhhhhh!" I yelled at the top of my lungs. The pain was unbelievable. Never before in my life had I felt pain like this.

Then a medium-built man came over and told the crowd to back up and leave me alone. A woman with him came over, propped me up, and held a cup of tea to my lips while photographers snapped pictures of me.

As the crowd quieted down and started to disperse, uniformed soldiers arrived and threw me on a stretcher and into a green truck. Bouncing along the road, I was in severe pain as they took me to a prison camp in the center of Hanoi.

They threw me into a cell at the prison, still on my stretcher and dressed only in my skivvies. Soon, a medical technician came in and bandaged up my wounds without saying a word. Following that, a mean-looking interrogator arrived.

"You are a war criminal in my country," he yelled at me.

I shook my head in disagreement.

"What is your name?" he asked.

I gave him my name, rank, serial number, and date of birth. I could tell he wasn't satisfied with that. He wanted more.

"What kind of plane do you fly?" he said more forcefully.

I didn't answer.

"What are your future targets?" he continued.

Again, I just stared at him.

Furious, he stood up and said, "If you give me information, you will receive medical treatment."

I didn't believe him. "I'm not going to give you anything," I replied politely.

He abruptly kicked me in the stomach and left. The pain from his foot immediately set in, and my world went dark.

For the next four days, the interrogations and beatings continued. I refused to give up any information and subsequently took the pounding for my non-cooperation. After each beating, I blacked out.

Later on the fourth day, two guards came back. One pulled back my blanket to show the other guard my injury. I looked at my knee. It was about the size and shape of a football.

"Okay, get the officer," I said in a panicked voice.

An officer came in a few minutes later. He looked like a Bug with his beady little red eyes. I enjoyed making the enemy into animals. It gave me some satisfaction.

"You want to talk now?" the Bug asked.

I replied, "I'll give you military information if you take me to the hospital."

Immediately, he left and came back with a doctor. "His name is Zorba," he said, pointing to the doc.

I could tell Zorba was completely incompetent. He squatted down and took my pulse, shaking his head and babbling to Bug.

"Are you going to take me to the hospital?" I asked.

The Bug replied, "It's too late."

"If you take me to the hospital, I'll get well," I responded.

Zorba took my pulse a second time and shook his head again.

"It's too late," Bug said again, and both men got up and left.

Sometime later, the Bug came rushing into the room, shouting, "Your father is a big admiral; now we take you to the hospital."

At the hospital, a doctor attempted to set my right arm, which was broken in three places. I passed out in the operating room since I received no anesthesia.

I was in a plaster cast from my waist to my neck when I awoke. I could tell from the cast that my arm was not set correctly and floated freely inside the plaster.

"You need another operation," the doctor said. "Your arm is still no good."

With the cast still wet, they moved me into a clean room. A distinguished North Vietnamese man who looked like a "Cat" awaited me. I could tell he was a high-ranking military official by his uniform.

"Lieutenant McCain, a French photographer named Chalais, is here to film you," he said.

"I don't want to be filmed," I replied bluntly.

"You need two operations, and if you don't talk to him, then we will take your chest cast off, and you won't get any operations," he responded. "You will say you're grateful to the Vietnamese people and are sorry for your crimes."

I shook my head and said, "I won't do it."

The Cat motioned for the door, and a French man walked in. After a few meaningless questions, the Cat became angry and stopped filming.

"You will demand an end to the war," he yelled at me, grabbing my broken arm.

"No, I'm not going to say anything else," I fired back.

Chalais broke in and said, "I'm satisfied with everything."

"You will tell them—" the Bug said.

"Colonel, I've got everything I need." Chalais interrupted again.

The Cat stopped twisting my arm.

"John, how's the prison food?" Chalais inquired.

"Well, it's okay, but it's not Paris," I said, trying to make small talk.

The French man smiled and left.

The Cat was not happy and followed behind him.

I was transferred four weeks later, stretcher and all, to "The Plantation," another prison in Hanoi. Two guards hoisted me into a small cell with two other Americans.

After the guards left, one of the men came over and said, "Hi, I'm Major George Day, but you can call me "Bud"' and this is Major Norris Overly," pointing to the other man.

"Glad to meet ya; I'm John McCain, Navy A-4 pilot."

Motioning to my cast, Bud said, "Kid, you're in some kind of bad shape."

"They tried to set my arm, but I know they messed it up," I replied.

Unable to sit up, Bud fed me some rice and water. Then I blanked out and slept until the next day.

When the sun rose, Norris took a bucket of water and did his best to clean me up. I could tell my weight was down about fifty pounds since I had ejected from my aircraft. My strength was gone, and it took everything I had to stay awake.

After a few months, my strength returned with Bud and Norris's help. I was finally able to put on some weight. Days turned into weeks, and months into years. Time had no meaning for me as I waited for the war to end.

Five and a half years later, I knew the war's end was near. A guard came in and transferred me into a cell with other prisoners who were captured at the same time as I was. My spirits increased as everybody in my group knew they were preparing to return us.

The next day, a guard said, "Tomorrow, you go home. Tonight, big meal for you."

I thought it was typical of the North Vietnamese. The food was horrible for the entire time I had been in prison. Then the night before I was to go home, they prepared a big meal for us.

The next day there was no special ceremony as we prepared to leave. The International Control Commission arrived before we left and looked around. They took a lot of photographs, but that was it.

Then a long line of buses pulled up, and the camp director told us to get in. Until now, I tried not to allow myself to be too hopeful. I had been tricked many times in the past, thinking I was going to be released.

At Gia Lam Airport, I shook hands with an American, and I knew it was over. Excitement filled my blood veins as I boarded a US Air Force plane. Taking one last look at Vietnam, I felt like I'd been to hell and back.

John and Carol McCain were reunited on St. Patrick's Day 1973 in Jacksonville, Florida. Unbeknownst to John, Carol had been in a severe car crash in 1969 in which her legs, pelvis, and arm were crushed. Even his oldest son Doug showed up on crutches with a broken leg from soccer. Nothing has ever stopped John McCain, and I believe nothing ever will.

ACKNOWLEDGMENTS

Pilots of Valor stories were revised from the following articles. Their intense research has made this book possible.

1 . Captain Merlyn Hans Dethlefsen, rewritten from Air Force Heroes in Vietnam by Major Donald K. Schneider, 1985.

2 . Major Leo K. Thorsness, rewritten from Air Force Heroes in Vietnam by Major Donald K. Schneider, 1985.

3 . Lt. Col. Joe M. Jackson, rewritten from Air Force Heroes in Vietnam by Major Donald K. Schneider, 1985.

4 . Captain Gerald O. Young, rewritten from Air Force Heroes in Vietnam by Major Donald K. Schneider, 1985.

5 . 1st Lt. James P. Fleming, rewritten from Air Force Heroes in Vietnam by Major Donald K. Schneider, 1985.

6 . Major Bernard F. Fisher, rewritten from Air Force Heroes in Vietnam by Major Donald K. Schneider, 1985.

7 . Captain Steven L. Bennett, rewritten from Air Force Heroes in Vietnam by Major Donald K. Schneider, 1985.

8 . Captains Bob Pardo and Earl Aman, rewritten from Airman magazine, December 1996.

9 . Lt. Colonel William A. Jones III, rewritten from Air Force Heroes in Vietnam by Major Donald K. Schneider, 1985.

10. Captain Hilliard A. Wilbanks, rewritten from Air Force Heroes in Vietnam by Major Donald K. Schneider, 1985.

11. 1st Lieutenant Leon Crane, rewritten from Flying Safety magazine, July 1990.

12. CW2 Daniel R. Smee and CW4 Franklin C. Harrison, rewritten from Flying Safety magazine, October 1995.

13. Anonymous, rewritten from Flying Safety magazine, October 1989.

14. Major Michael G. Shook was rewritten from Combat Edge in November 1994.

15. Major Chuck Foster and Captain Brett Hartnett rewritten from Flying Safety magazine, August 1994.

16. Captain Brian Udell, rewritten from Airman magazine, April 1997.

17. Lieutenant James M. Leavis, rewritten from Flying Safety, April 1997.

18. Master Sergeant Wayne Issacson, rewritten from Combat Crew, May 1991.

19. Captain Lance Peter Sijan, rewritten from Airman magazine, January 1996, and Air Force Heroes in Vietnam by Major Donald K. Schneider, 1985.

20. Lt. Commander John S. McCain III, rewritten from US News & World Report, Inc., May 14, 1973.

ABOUT THE AUTHORS

Major Don Pickinpaugh was a Lockheed U-2S Instructor Pilot at Beale Air Force Base in California. He was the Assistant Director of Operations for the 1st Reconnaissance Squadron. Major Pickinpaugh also served as a T-37 Instructor Pilot for four years at Reese Air Force Base, Texas. He has over 2,300 flying hours in U-2s, T-38s, and T-37s. He is married to the former Sherri Juall of East Lansing, Michigan.

Don't miss out!

Visit the website below and you can sign up to receive emails whenever Donald Pickinpaugh publishes a new book. There's no charge and no obligation.

https://books2read.com/r/B-A-BRUX-UYJIC

Connecting independent readers to independent writers.

About the Author

Major Don Pickinpaugh was a Lockheed U-2S Instructor Pilot at Beale Air Force Base in California. He was the Assistant Director of Operations for the 1st Reconnaissance Squadron. Major Pickinpaugh also served as a T-37 Instructor Pilot for four years at Reese Air Force Base, Texas. He has over 2,300 flying hours in U-2s, T-38s, and T-37s. Don logged 36 combat hours during Desert Storm. He is married to the former Sherri Juall of East Lansing, Michigan.